Domino 7 Application Development

Writing and upgrading applications for the latest
Lotus Notes / Domino Platform

Dick McCarrick

Stephen Cooke

Timothy Speed

Raphael Savir

BIRMINGHAM - MUMBAI

Domino 7 Application Development

First published: January 2007

Production Reference: 1220107

Published by Packt Publishing Ltd.
32 Lincoln Road
Olton
Birmingham, B27 6PA, UK.

ISBN 978-1-904811-06-0

www.packtpub.com

Cover Image by www.visionwt.com

Warning and Disclaimer

The authors have attempted to ensure the contents of this book are as complete and accurate as possible, but no warranty of fitness is implied regarding any information and/or products referenced in this book. Several of the authors, at the time of publishing, were employees of IBM. The IBM Corporation provides a set of rules regarding publishing that applies to each employee. The IBM employees followed each of these rules as stated by IBM. Based on those rules, be advised that:

- This book is not sponsored by IBM/Lotus or ISSL.
- The IBM employees received IBM's legal permission to publish this book, using an outside IBM Press publisher.
- All users of this book do so at their own risk.
- The products referenced or mentioned in this book are listed for informational purposes only. The publisher and authors may have received demo copies to review. Several different vendors are mentioned in this book, and vendor products are used for reference. The publisher and authors do not recommend any product, software, or hardware. You, the owner of your hardware, software, and data, are responsible to make a determination of what is best for you. The authors do advise that you take careful consideration in determining your software, security, and infrastructure needs, and review more than just one vendor.

Domino 7 is a great product with many new features. If you find an error, please let us know.

IBM

The IBM list of copyrights and trademarks can be found at `http://www.ibm.com/legal/copytrade.shtml`.

In no event will IBM be liable to any party for any direct, indirect, special, or other consequential damages for any use of this book. All information is provided by the authors on an "as is" basis only. IBM provides no representations and warranties, express or implied, including the implied warranties of fitness for a particular purpose, merchantability and non-infringement for any information in this book.

Credits

Authors

Dick McCarrick

Stephen Cooke

Timothy Speed

Raphael Savir

Reviewer

Barry Heinz

Development Editor

David Barnes

Assistant Development Editor

Nikhil Bangera

Technical Editors

Divya Menon

Saurabh Singh

Editorial Manager

Dipali Chittar

Project Manager

Patricia Weir

Project Coordinator

Suneet Amrute

Indexer

Bhushan Pangaonkar

Proofreaders

Martin Brooks

Chris Smith

Layouts and Illustrations

Manjiri Nadkarni

Shantanu Zagade

Cover Designer

Shantanu Zagade

Foreword

Congratulations on investing your time to learn more about Lotus Notes and Domino! This book comes at a key time for Notes/Domino application developers and their organizations.

Since its introduction, Notes/Domino has been a true collaboration platform for businesses. It has uniquely combined collaboration with business applications—all within the context of what users are trying to accomplish. A powerful programming platform combined with intuitive tools, it opened up many business ideas and processes to automation through millions of applications, from small personal tools to mission-critical, line-of-business systems. It has also led to the establishment of one of the most creative and largest developer communities in the industry.

A review of Notes/Domino through the years shows how it has revolutionized the way we work. See also the article, "*The History of Notes and Domino*", published on the developerWorks: Lotus website (www.ibm.com/developerworks/lotus/library/ls-NDHistory). The 35,000 users who adopted Notes Version 1 got the first look at many of the features that we take for granted today, including mail, discussion databases, group directories, customizable applications, Access Control Lists (ACLs), doclinks, encryption, and replication to name just a few. When released, these were all revolutionary new concepts that allowed users to be more productive.

Release 2 focused on scalability issues, allowing Notes to support roughly 10,000 users and accommodate larger enterprises. This release also included enhancements to the application programming interface (API), mail (including return receipt, address look-up, and multiple address books), and additional formula language functionality.

By the time Release 3 was introduced, nearly 500,000 people used Notes. To make the user experience better for the growing user base, Release 3 focused on improving the user interface, further enhancing scalability, as well as incorporating features such as full-text search, selective replication, and support for the Mac client.

With Release 4, the world was introduced to a highly revamped version of Notes, one designed to embrace Internet technology by integrating Notes with the Web. In addition to a completely redesigned user interface, people were introduced to

Internet integration that allowed Web-browser accessible Notes databases, new messaging capabilities, and the LotusScript programming language.

Release 5 furthered the concept of Web integration, and also gave users a browser-type interface with a customizable Welcome page. For application developers, Domino Designer provided a conducive environment for creating secure applications.

Release 6 represented a significant step towards integrating Notes with the rest of the IBM software portfolio. Two features that customers especially embraced were the integration of Sametime instant messaging into the Notes client, and the ability to access mail from the Web. Enhancements were also made to Domino Designer to make it easier to create applications and reuse code.

With more than 125 million users worldwide, Release 7 of Notes/Domino was notable for many reasons, including significant improvements in the user interface, scalability, and the total cost of ownership. However, the most powerful and important set of changes occurred in the programming model. Capabilities were added to allow Notes applications to utilize Web Services and a relational data store (DB2).

The underlying reason for these changes is very simple: Notes and Domino applications represent a huge investment for customers. It has become critical for applications to be able to be leveraged, integrated, and reused. Increasingly, this means allowing these applications to participate in loosely coupled standards-based architectures. Service-Oriented Architecture (SOA) has become the prevailing term for this type of implementation.

Many customers I talk to do not yet think of their Notes and Domino applications as potential elements in an SOA strategy. I think that is a mistake. This book is a great resource to help you start thinking about SOA, and how it should relate to your Notes environment.

So what's next?

As this book nears publication, Notes 8 (announced with the code name Hannover) is progressing into its first public beta. Many observers have commented on the exponential progress that has been made in the user experience, or the integration of activity-centric computing. These are certainly critical elements and will be a key differentiator for Notes 8. But something deeper lies beneath the surface for application developers. With Notes 8 being based on a Java-based Eclipse foundation, developers have new options. Not only can you continue to run and develop traditional Notes applications (unchanged!), you can start to build composite applications that are enterprise mashups of Java components, .nsf-based applications, data delivered via portlets, or other components that can be hosted within an Eclipse plug-in (such as .Net). Also, for the first time, Notes and Sametime (with Version 7.5) will share a common foundation allowing sharing of application components.

So, everything you have still runs, and you can adopt multiple programming models at your pace. Why does this matter? Because:

- Your existing applications and skills investment are protected and can easily be extended to build a new generation of open applications.
- Notes will provide a rich client for not only Domino, but Portal or Java-based applications. Essentially, Notes will become the client for SOA.
- The Notes development community will have the potential for significant growth as Notes becomes a viable deployment platform for the millions of developers working with Eclipse and Java.

Applications in the context of business processes have never been more important. In some ways, we are coming right back to the original value proposition of Notes.

So Notes is new again. Enjoy this book for what it can help you deliver now—and start thinking about what the future can hold!

On a personal note, I'd like to extend my congratulations to the authors. Their collective skill is in constant demand by customers around the world. Writing this book is a labor of love and a huge contribution to the Lotus community.

Congratulations!

Alistair Rennie
VP, Software Services
Lotus

About the Authors

Dick McCarrick is a freelance technical writer. He is co-author of the book *Upgrading to Lotus Notes and Domino 7*, aimed at Lotus Notes/Domino end users and administrators. Previously Dick worked for Lotus/IBM for over 15 years, first as a member of the Notes/Domino Documentation team and later for the developerWorks Lotus (LDD) website. At Lotus/IBM, he played a variety of roles in documenting many major components of Domino and Notes. He also wrote and edited numerous technical articles, including the regular column, "Ask Professor INI."

In his spare time, Dick's leisure activities include running, fishing, woodworking, and reading about the natural sciences. An avid astronomer, he is former director of the Bridgewater (Mass.) State College Observatory.

I would like to thank my wife Lisa for her unflagging support, both for my career and my life in general.

Stephen Cooke began programming as a hobbyist on the Apple. He later became involved with PCs in a professional capacity while working in the Czech Republic. He went on to work for Notes CS, a Lotus Business Partner in Prague. He has twelve years of consulting experience and has been working for IBM since 2000. He currently focuses on helping customers with Lotus and WebSphere-related challenges. His written work has also appeared in IBM developerWorks.

I would like to thank Tim Speed for the invitation to participate in this book, and my family for their patience and encouragement. I would also like to thank the folks at Teamstudio for their quick response to requests for information, and the people whose efforts went into preparing this book for publication.

Timothy Speed is an infrastructure and security architect for IBM Software Services for Lotus (ISSL). Tim has been involved in Internet and messaging security since 1992. Tim also participated with the Domino infrastructure at the Nagano Olympics and assisted with the Lotus Notes systems for the Sydney Olympics. His certifications include MCSE©, CISSP, Lotus Domino CLP Principal Administrator, and Lotus Domino CLP Principal Developer. Tim also is certified in Domino ND6 and D7. Tim has also co-authored six books: *The Internet Security Guidebook* (ISBN: 0122374711); *The Personal Internet Security Guidebook* (ISBN: 0126565619); *Enterprise Directory and Security Implementation Guide: Designing and Implementing Directories in Your Organization* (ISBN: 0121604527); *Internet Security: A Jumpstart for Systems Administrators and IT Managers* (ISBN: 1555582982); *SSL VPN: Understanding, Evaluating and Planning Secure, Web-based Remote Access* (ISBN: 1904811078); and *Upgrading to Lotus Notes and Domino 7* (ISBN: 1904811639).

Knowledge is based on many different facets—what you know, knowing where information can be found, and who you know. The information in this book is a combination of all these facets. Data sources have been referenced in this book, these include references to people, URLs, and other books. But much of the knowledge that is in this book comes from very smart people. First and foremost I need to thank my wife for helping me with the book and providing some of the editing throughout the various chapters. I thank my daughter Katherine for tolerating me during the months that I worked on this book. I am very grateful to Dick McCarrick for being crazy enough to coauthor this book. Special thanks to David Barnes the Development Editor. Also, thanks to Lotus/IBM (and ISSL), Walter Larry Berthelsen, and Jack Shoemaker for allowing me to coauthor this book. Thanks to Barry Heinz for reading/reviewing this book before publishing. Thanks to the content authors Dick McCarrick and Stephen Cooke.

To Linda Speed—"just me"

Garry White (a great educator and technologist), Lillian Speed, Joe Christopher, Ted Smith, Gail Pilgrim (sorry I forgot you in the last book), Bob Stegmaier, Charles DeLone, Kevin Mills, Boris Vishnevsky, Brad Schauf, Chris Cotton, David Byrd, Kathrine Rutledge, Charles Carrington, Mark Harper, Jordi Riera, David Via, Heidi Wulkow, Dave Erickson, David Bell, Mark Leaser, John Kistler, Jon P Dodge, Luc Groleau, Zena Washington, Burk Buechler, Robert Thietje, Francois Nasser, Marlene Botter, Roy Hudson, Mike Dudding, Ciaran DellaFera, Tom Agoston, Carl Baumann, Shane Geoge, Tery W. Corkran, David Hinkle, Don Nadel, Doug Parham,

Ed Brill, Gary Ernst, Steve Keohane, Steven Kramer, Gregg Smith, Hartmut Samtleben, Hissan C Waheed, Ian Reid, John Norton, Katherine Emling, Kevin Lynch, Marc Galeazza, Mark Steinborn, Mary Ellen Zurko, Matthew Milza, Matthew Speed, Peter Burkhardt, Ralph Vawter, Sherry Price, Stephen Hardison, Laurie Jones, Christopher Byrne, Steve Matrullo, Marco M Noel, Kelly M Ryan, David Ryan, Alex Dobrovodsky, Alistair Rennie, Andy Higgins, Todd Merkel, Butch Bantug, Carlos Gonzalez, Chad Holznagel, Deyhle, Dave, Steve Sterka, Dolby Linwood, Jason Short, Tracy Goddard, Frederic Dahm, Gary Desmarais, Gary Palmer, Glenn Sicam, Sean F Moore, Jeff Bryant, James Gallece, Shaker Al-Muaber, Dr. John Lamb, Kim Armstrong , Lance Haverly, Lisa Santana, Stewart Nichols, Nancy Long, Bryan Bradsby, Robert Hamnik, Wouter Aukema, Robert Nellis, Trenton Kelley, William Destache, and Chuck Stauber.

Finally, sorry if I missed you on this book, I will get you in the next. Sorry, Circe, you don't get an acknowledgment in this book.

Raphael Savir has been a developer and consultant for Lotus Notes/Domino applications for 15 years. He has worked in numerous positions, focusing on performance and development topics. Raphael enjoys speaking on these topics, and has been fortunate in being able to do so frequently over the years.

Now with LS Development Corporation (`http://www.lsdevelopment.com`), Raphael works directly with clients to make efficient and friendly Notes or web applications running on the Domino platform. Raphael has written several development articles over the years, but this is his first attempt to string together more than a few pages.

I would like to thank my beautiful and encouraging wife, Lizzie, for helping me get through a brutal year of work and writing.

About the Reviewer

Barry Heinz is a Senior IT Architect with the IBM Software Group, specializing in Lotus software for large enterprises. He has been working with Lotus Notes and Domino since 1992.

Table of Contents

Preface

If you're reading this book, you're probably already familiar with the Domino server. You know about all the powerful productivity features offered by this product and you know how much your company relies on it to communicate, collaborate, and manage its collective store of corporate knowledge.

This book is intended to help you with developing applications on the latest release of the Domino platform. This book has been written by Notes/Domino 'insiders'. Collectively, we possess decades of Notes/Domino experience; we've been with the product since Notes 1.0, and since then have worked directly with customers to help them with their Notes/Domino upgrade and deployment issues.

What This Book Covers

Chapters 1 and 2 will help you understand the new features in Notes and Domino 7.

Chapter 3 shows how to use DB2 as a data store for Domino databases so as to bring the scalability features of DB2 and the flexibility of SQL into Domino applications. The chapter shows how to install, configure, map, and then access Domino data stored in DB2.

Chapter 4 will show you how to make the best use of new features added in Domino Designer 7 to better manage Lotus Notes and Domino applications. Specifically we will be covering Autosave, Agent Profiling, and remote Java debugging.

Chapter 5 shows how to ensure that critical applications continue to run smoothly after you upgrade your Notes/Domino installation, while taking advantage of the new features and functionality release 7 has to offer.

Chapter 6 will tackle issues you need to consider when upgrading your @Formula language to Notes/Domino. We first detail a backup strategy and then take a tour through the new Notes/Domino @Formulas and the potential upgrade issues they raise.

Chapter 7 runs through the process of upgrading Domino-based agents and LotusScript; we also cover the use of TeamStudio Analyzer, which is a third-party tool to assist with your upgrade. The second half of the chapter runs through the new features available to LotusScript developers in Domino Designer 7.

Chapter 8 examines Domino-based web services and you will see the Java implementation of one such web service. We cover the various tools Domino Designer 7 provides for interacting with WSDL and finish by examining the role UDDI plays in facilitating the adoption of web services.

Chapter 9 covers using best practices to optimize your Domino applications for performance; specifically we will see how to efficiently code database properties, views, and forms/agents to work well in a Domino environment.

In *Chapter 10*, you will learn to use the new programming features offered in Lotus Notes/Domino 7 by actually implementing them in code.

In *Chapter 11*, we will examine two important new features, Domino Domain Monitoring (DDM) and Agent Profiles, which are critical for troubleshooting your Notes/Domino applications. Additionally, the chapter runs through several tips and techniques for identifying and correcting problems in your Notes/Domino 7 applications.

In *Appendix A*, we review several vendor tools that you can use to help upgrade your applications to Lotus Notes/Domino 7. These include Angkor by Atlantic Decisions, PistolStar Password Power 8 Plug-ins by PistolStar, Inc, CMT Inspector from Binary Tree, and FT Search Manager from IONET.

Conventions

In this book, you will find a number of styles of text that distinguish between different kinds of information. Here are some examples of these styles, and an explanation of their meaning.

There are three styles for code. Code words in text are shown as follows: "The requirements of the `DiscoverFolders` command generally dictate that it be used from within a frameset."

A block of code will be set as follows:

```
@If(@AdminECLIsLocked; @Return("Administration ECL Is Locked");
@EditECL("Engineering" : "names.nsf"; "Testers"))
```

When we wish to draw your attention to a particular part of a code block, the relevant lines or items will be made bold:

```
GET_UNREAD_NOTE_TABLE: 600 ms
OPEN_COLLECTION(REP85256055:004781F8-NTFFFF0020,0040,0000)
OPEN_DB(CN=HQ/OU=Boston/O=Acme!!Applications\SalesTracking.nsf):
(Connect to HQ/Boston/Acme: 5000 ms)
GET_UNREAD_NOTE_TABLE: 4000 ms
RCV_UNREAD 2000 ms
```

New terms and **important words** are introduced in a bold-type font. Words that you see on the screen, in menus or dialog boxes for example, appear in our text like this: "clicking the **Next** button moves you to the next screen".

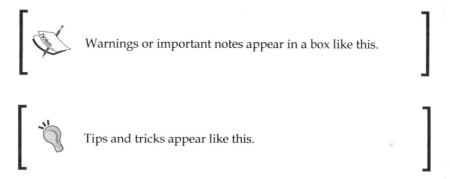

Warnings or important notes appear in a box like this.

Tips and tricks appear like this.

Reader Feedback

Feedback from our readers is always welcome. Let us know what you think about this book, what you liked or may have disliked. Reader feedback is important for us to develop titles that you really get the most out of.

To send us general feedback, simply drop an email to feedback@packtpub.com, making sure to mention the book title in the subject of your message.

If there is a book that you need and would like to see us publish, please send us a note in the **SUGGEST A TITLE** form on www.packtpub.com or email suggest@packtpub.com.

If there is a topic that you have expertise in and you are interested in either writing or contributing to a book, see our author guide on www.packtpub.com/authors.

Customer Support

Now that you are the proud owner of a Packt book, we have a number of things to help you to get the most from your purchase.

Downloading the Example Code for the Book

Visit http://www.packtpub.com/support, and select this book from the list of titles to download any example code or extra resources for this book. The files available for download will then be displayed.

 The downloadable files contain instructions on how to use them.

Errata

Although we have taken every care to ensure the accuracy of our contents, mistakes do happen. If you find a mistake in one of our books—maybe a mistake in text or code—we would be grateful if you would report this to us. By doing this you can save other readers from frustration, and help to improve subsequent versions of this book. If you find any errata, report them by visiting http://www.packtpub.com/support, selecting your book, clicking on the **Submit Errata** link, and entering the details of your errata. Once your errata have been verified, your submission will be accepted and the errata added to the list of existing errata. The existing errata can be viewed by selecting your title from http://www.packtpub.com/support.

Questions

You can contact us at questions@packtpub.com if you are having a problem with some aspect of the book, and we will do our best to address it.

1
A Short History of Notes and Domino

 In this chapter we will look into the history of Notes and Domino. Readers who have the *Upgrading to Lotus Notes and Domino 7* book from Packt publishing can skip Chapters 1 and 2 as they are similar to the introductory chapters from that book.

The genesis of Notes and Domino has achieved a near legendary status within the history of software development. Three middle-American college boys in the late 1970s wanted a way to share information. So they utilized a bug-reporting software program called PLATO Group Notes, which ran on their mainframe-based college computer system. This program would be considered archaic compared to modern day business programs, but it was an improvement upon the traditional swapping of handwritten notes hastily scribbled during classroom lectures. And it provided just enough communication and collaboration functionality to offer a hint as to what more could be done, given the right software and technology.

After graduation, these three students, whose names need no introduction to long-time members of the Lotus Notes community (but we'll mention them anyway, in case you're a newcomer: Ray Ozzie, Tim Halvorsen, and Len Kawell), went their separate ways. But none forgot the potential he saw in PLATO Group Notes. Halvorsen and Kawell took jobs at Digital Equipment Corporation, where they eventually created an in-house communication tool that resembled PLATO. Meanwhile, Ozzie took programming positions with other corporations, but never lost sight of his vision to form his own company and develop a more advanced, PC-based collaboration program. Eventually (1984 to be exact), with funding provided by Lotus Development Corporation (makers of the famous Lotus 1-2-3), Ozzie founded Iris Associates Inc. to develop the first release of Lotus Notes. Ozzie was soon joined by former classmates Halvorsen and Kawell, followed shortly by Steve Beckhardt.

When describing the software they created, the focus is usually on the end-user features provided by Lotus Notes, with a secondary nod to the server/administration component. Indeed, Lotus Notes has always been described as a client/server application, indicative of its "dual citizenship," with some of its functions performed locally on the user's PC and other functions done on the server. But from the beginning, the creators of Lotus Notes showed great foresight in recognizing that their product would not be an out-of-the-box application, a radical approach back in the early 1980s. Instead, they realized that Lotus Notes needed to be extremely customizable and flexible, and from its inception built these capabilities into Lotus Notes. (The fact that they did would eventually result in a large array of Notes custom applications, a growing demand for Notes application developers, and ultimately…this book!)

This first version of Lotus Notes was modelled on PLATO Group Notes, but was far more advanced, sporting powerful features such as on-line discussion, email, phone books, and document databases. This functionality presented some serious challenges to the hardware and supporting infrastructure upon which Notes ran at the time. To meet these challenges, Notes was built upon the previously mentioned client/server architecture that featured PCs connected to a **local area network** (**LAN**). Groups set up a dedicated server PC that communicated with other servers. These servers exchanged information through **replicated data**, a concept familiar to us today, but extremely revolutionary at that time. This allowed users to exchange information with co-workers (however remote), while maintaining high performance.

And as we mentioned, Notes, from the outset, was designed to be highly customizable, with a state-of-the-art multi-faceted programmatic interface that allowed developers to create powerful applications specifically suited to the needs of their workgroups. These programmatic features allowed developers with virtually any level of experience to put together applications. For example, Notes shipped with application templates (for example, address book, document library, and discussion database) that, with a little modification, could be used by most sites. (Many of us first got our "feet wet" with Notes development this way.) More experienced developers could use the development interface to build their own applications from scratch, creating their own fields, forms, and other components, and laying them out as they saw fit. And advanced programmers could take advantage of @functions to do really cool stuff, using Notes to solve business problems that advanced the scope and vision of the product. All these features helped Notes to become adopted as an essential tool for many businesses (and not incidentally, soon led to the growth of a large and lively business-partner community).

The first release of Notes shipped in 1989. (A five-year development cycle may seem like a long time by today's standards, but bear in mind, the Iris folks were basically creating an entirely new genre of software.)

Release 1.0 features included:

- Email
- Advanced security features, which included the now-familiar Access Control Lists (ACLs). Other security-related features included encryption, signing, and authentication using the RSA public-key technology. All these features gave application developers a variety of tools to help ensure their applications were secure yet readily accessible to the right users
- Dial-up functionality
- Import/export capability, including Lotus Freelance Graphics metafile import, structured ASCII export, and Lotus 1-2-3/Symphony export
- Online help (a novel idea at the time!)
- Formula language for programming Notes applications
- DocLinks that allowed users to navigate from one Notes document to another, via technology that resembled an early form of today's URLs
- Central administration

Notes 2.0 shipped in 1991. By now, it became apparent that much of Notes' early customer base consisted of large companies that employed thousands of users. These companies were particularly intrigued by Notes' ability to bring large numbers of users together, and allow them to collaborate and share information with the speed and efficiency of a small, tightly-focused team. And they loved the built-in ability to adapt Notes templates to their specific needs, and/or build their own applications from scratch. To accommodate these customers, the Notes development team paid special attention to scalability enhancements, taking advantage of recent hardware and networking advances that could support large, geographically dispersed environments. These scalability features included support for multiple Name and Address books.

For developers, the addition of a Notes C Applications Programming Interface (API) enhanced Notes' extensibility, allowing experienced programmers to create more advanced custom applications. The formula language was also extended. And on the user side, Notes now supported rich text.

Notes 3.0 shipped in mid-1993. At this point, the installed customer base for the product had grown to approximately half a million users worldwide—substantial, but still orders of magnitude smaller than today's global Notes/Domino community. To help broaden its appeal to new markets, Notes 3.0 offered client support for the Apple Macintosh and server support for Microsoft Windows. Notes 3.0 also introduced many now-familiar features, including:

- Full-text search
- Hierarchical names

- Alternate mail
- Enhanced replication that allowed users to perform selective replication, and run replication in the background

It was around this time that the Internet began drawing attention as a serious business tool, rather than merely the domain of students and socially inept "geeks". This led to the release of InterNotes News, a product that provided a gateway between the Internet news sources and Notes. Although largely forgotten today, this was the first project that reflected the increasing need for Notes to work together with the Internet.

In January 1996, Lotus released Notes 4.0, offering a radically redesigned user interface that simplified many Notes features, making it easier to use, program, and administer. This interface quickly became popular among users and developers. The product continued to become faster and more scalable. In addition, Notes began to integrate with the Web, and many new features reflected emerging web technology. For instance, the new Server Web Navigator allowed the Notes servers to retrieve pages off the Web, allowing users to view the pages in a Notes client.

Release 4.0 included something for everybody, especially application developers. As we mentioned, the user interface was completely re-engineered, offering the familiar three-paned UI (with preview capability) for mail and other applications. This UI is still available today in the Notes workspace. Users also took advantage of the enhanced search features, which included the ability to search non-indexed databases. Programmers welcomed the introduction of LotusScript, a programming language built into Notes, as well as new view, folder, and design features.

Administrators also had a lot to cheer about. For example, the introduction of "pass-thru" servers made it much easier to build network topologies that ensured quick SOCKS support, HTTP proxy support, and Notes RPC proxy support.

In July 1995, IBM purchased Lotus. This gave the Notes developer team access to world-class technology, including the HTTP server now known as Domino (which eventually led to the Notes product being known by the current name Notes/Domino). This helped transform the Notes 4.0 server into an interactive web-application server, combining the open networking environment of Internet standards and protocols with the powerful application development facilities of Notes. These features made Notes an important web-application development platform. And the Domino server allowed customers to dynamically publish Notes documents to the Web. This was a major development in the life of the product.

Among the major enhancements offered in release 4.5 was Calendar and Scheduling (hard to believe it hasn't been in the product all along). And to further the theme of web integration (which began with Notes 4.0), release 4.5 also included:

- Personal Web Navigator, along with seamless web access from the Notes client

- Improved scalability and manageability with Domino server clusters and directory assistance

- Security enhancements, such as Execution Control Lists, and password expiration and reuse. This helped give users more control over who could access their PCs and what could be performed on them

- And for the programming community, Notes/Domino 4.5 introduced script libraries

Notes and Domino release 5.0 shipped in early 1999. "R5" (as it was widely known) continued the theme of Notes/Domino integration with the Web to the point where the two technologies were inseparable. This was reflected in the R5 interface, which bore a more browser-like feel. This release also supported more Internet standards and protocols. And the new Domino Administrator made Domino network administration easier.

But what many in the Notes/Domino application development community remember most about R5 was the introduction of Domino Designer, the third member of the Notes/Domino triumvirate of products. Although (as we've shown) development features and capabilities have always been an integral part of Notes, the elevation of these features to separate product status was an important demonstration of just how versatile and valuable Notes/Domino had become as an application development platform, especially for web users.

Notes/Domino 5.0 featured:

- Internet messaging and directories
- Expanded web-application services (including CORBA)
- Database improvements, such as transaction logging

The Notes 5.0 client included a new browser-like user interface with a customizable welcome page for tracking daily information. It also included improvements to applications such as mail, calendar and scheduling, web browsing, and discussions.

By the time Notes 6.0 and Domino 6.0 were introduced in late 2002, industry talk focused on concepts such as lower total cost of ownership (TCO for the buzzword-inclined), increased productivity, and quicker deployment; in other words, doing more with less, and faster.

In response, Domino 6.0 offered enhanced installation, scalability, and performance. Domino Designer 6.0 allowed developers to create complex applications more easily and to reuse code. And IBM improved the Notes 6.0 client, with an eye towards increasing each user's personal productivity. The overarching theme was to help customers work more efficiently. For example, installation and setup offered more options and an improved interface. Domino 6.0 made central management of multiple remote servers easier through features such as policy-based management. And it improved server scalability and performance, with new features such as network compression and Domino Server Monitor. These themes were carried through Notes/Domino 6.5, which offered enhanced collaboration with tighter integration with Sametime, QuickPlace, and Domino Web Access.

For programmers, release 6.5 included the Lotus Domino Toolkit for WebSphere Studio, a set of Eclipse plug-ins you can use to create JavaServer Pages (JSPs) using the Domino Custom Tags.

That brings us to Notes/Domino 7. This latest release continues the tradition of cutting edge technology and functionality built into that first release of Lotus Notes. This is especially true for Domino Designer, which, as we discussed, has grown from a set of developer features in release 1 to a full-fledged application development product and platform. We discuss all the new features in Domino Designer 7 (and the upgrade issues they raise) later in this book. But before we do, let's take a quick look at the new client and administration features in Notes/Domino 7 to help us better understand all the facets of this release and how they work together.

Summary

This chapter took us through the progress of Notes and Domino from its initial stages to its latest version—Notes/Domino 7. The next chapter will quickly take us through Notes 7 and Domino 7 functionality.

2
New Notes 7 Client and Domino 7 Server Features

This book is of course aimed at the Notes/Domino application developer, and therefore its primary focus is on the new application development and programming features of Domino Designer 7 (and the related upgrade issues they may raise). However, the well-rounded developer should also have a working acquaintance with other areas of Notes/Domino 7, including the Notes client and Domino server. Keeping abreast of new and enhanced Notes 7 client features and functionality will help you understand what release 7 offers to your end users, to better prepare you for creating applications that deliver and compliment these new features. And being knowledgeable about the Domino 7 server can help you design applications that are more easily hosted, supported, and maintained by your server administrators.

So in this chapter, we present a short review of many of the new features in Notes and Domino 7. This includes new features in:

- Lotus Notes
- Domino Administrator
- Domino server
- LEI

The following sections briefly examine the major new features in all these products.

Lotus Notes 7

The Lotus Notes client includes a large set of new features. Details on these features are described in our previous book, *Upgrading to Lotus Notes and Domino 7*, from Packt Publishing. This section takes a quick review of many of these new features.

You can now, with a single click, close all open windows. Also, you can save the state of your work. Use this ability to save the window state for Lotus Notes to remember where you were working by permanently setting the window state to the currently opened windows.

Notes now offers the ability to be prompted when you send a message with no subject:

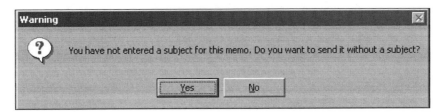

There are new client follow-up actions to help with messaging tracking and workflow. (This displays with the right mouse button.)

There are new mail rules for spam management. For those looking for a quick status on digital message signatures and encryption, there are new status bar icons that will display this status. And there are improved workspace wizards.

One of the best new client features is the ability to automatically save your work. This can be really be helpful in the event that your computer crashes and/or has a power loss. This feature will save the work so that you can retrieve it when the Lotus Notes client starts.

With Notes 7, you can sort by subject in your mail files. This option is available in the views **All Documents**, **Inbox**, **Sent**, **Drafts**, and others. Mail threads allow you to track a set of mail messages via the lifetime of that set of messages.

Notes 7 Calendar and Scheduling (C&S) includes a new Calendar Cleanup action that helps the end-user to quickly and easily maintain calendar entries.

Also with C&S, you can now set up the online portion of the meeting to restrict attendees to only those on the invite list. You can also provide a password for an online meeting. Other enhanced C&S support includes new options for managing rooms and resources. Now end-users can specify a preferred site and a preferred list of rooms and/or resources to use when scheduling meetings.

In addition, end-users can now configure the calendar to accept a meeting, even if it conflicts with an earlier meeting.

Calendar owners can also mark messages for follow up in mail files that they manage. And they are prompted to specify where forwarded mail is saved.

How about this scenario: you found the document you want, but how can you find what folders it is listed in? You can do this now with the ability to "discover" folders. When a document is selected in the view, and the **Folder | Discover Folders** action is selected, a dialog box will be displayed showing which folders the selected document is in.

Lotus Notes 7 also offers enhanced presence awareness based upon Lotus Sametime. End users can now see a person's name in a document or view and determine if that person is online. Presence awareness has been added to Team Rooms, Discussions, To Do documents, Personal Name and Address Book, Rooms and Resources templates, and various C&S views.

You can also access Notes mail through the Microsoft Office XP Smart Tags. Microsoft Office Smart Tags recognize certain types of text, for example, a person's name.

Notes 7 additionally includes improved Rooms and Resources usability (including a simple form to create a reservation and the ability to transfer a reservation), and improved email archiving.

Domino Administrator

There are several significant new features and improvements with release 7 of the Domino Administrator client. These new features will help administrators with configuration, maintenance, and uptime. One of the most important new features is Domino Domain Monitoring (DDM). Chapter 11 has a section dedicated to this new powerful feature. Other features/tools include administration event script handling (via LotusScript).

Policy administration has been enhanced. This includes the ability to lock down end-user desktops, and a new Mail policy.

Domino 7 provides integration with **Tivoli Autonomic Monitoring Engine (TAME)**. This provides event reporting capabilities to other Tivoli Interfaces (for example, Tivoli Enterprise Console). Domino resource modules, built for Domino TAME, can report CPU-, memory-, disk-, and network-utilization statistics. The resource modules are configured with DDM interfaces and report to Tivoli Enterprise Console.

The improved activity trends feature uses these Domino server features:

- Activity logging to collect information used for resource balancing.
- Activity trends to set up times for data collection and retention.
- Domino Change Manager to implement a workflow process in which changes made to the system are controlled and approved.

Enhancements to Smart Upgrade include the ability to detach kits in the background, to prevent time lost to a non-working client; and failover from a shared (network) upgrade kit to another server's attached kit. If clustered, Smart Upgrade uses a cluster mate if the first server is unavailable. Smart Upgrade also helps prevent excessive server load by limiting the number of downloads from a single server. Also, it provides notification to administrators, via a mail-in database, of the Smart Upgrade status by user/machine (Success, Failed, or Delayed). In addition, you can provision the Smart Upgrade Tracking database.

DB2 Management tools let you enable Domino to run with a DB2 data store, configure a connection document from DB2 Access for a Domino server to Domino, and allow DB2 usernames/passwords to be added to server IDs. You also have enhanced support in status and statistics panels indicating DB2 usage and statistics plus other visual cues. (See Chapter 3 for more on the new DB2 integration features offered in Notes/Domino 7.)

Other new features include:

- The ability to write status bar history to a log file.

- The ability to suppress the **Roaming User Upgrade** prompt.

- Domino Web Administrator support for Mozilla browsers.

- Three new event-notification methods, which are programmable via LotusScript, batch language, Java, C, and so on.

- An enhanced Message ID feature that allows a message ID to be prefixed to console messages, via the `notes.ini` settings `Display_MessageID=1` and `Display_MessageSeverity=1`.

The administration process will no longer revert name changes automatically, but will require that the administrator either approve or reject the name change reversion.

Domino Server

The Domino 7 server enhancements include autonomic diagnostic collection, a feature that can be considered both an administration feature as well as a server feature. This powerful feature is used to analyze various processes and events that are generated from a Notes client or Domino server after a crash. Autonomic diagnostic collection was first released with Notes and Domino 6.0.1. Be sure to take some time to understand and utilize this powerful tool.

Domino 7 includes more improvements to directories and LDAP; for example, support for Universal Notes IDs (UNID) through 32-character values of the new dominoUNID operational attribute. LDAP searches have been enhanced to work with IBM Workplace products that use the WebSphere Member Manager (WMM) service to access user/group objects. To optimize performance, Domino 7 re-uses existing LDAP connections, rather than initialize and close new ones for every user attempting to access protected resources whose credentials need to be verified in the external LDAP directory.

IPv6 protocol support has been upgraded to include additional platforms and services. CIDR format is now supported in IP address pattern strings. IOCP support in Linux Intel is included, as well as support for 1024-bit RSA and 128-bit RC2 Notes keys.

Administrators can limit how far into the future users can make reservations. Administrators can also set automatic reminder notices to be sent to the Chairperson who books a particular room/resource so that if a meeting is cancelled, the room/resource can be released. In addition, embedded graphics in the **Description** field now appear when you send an invitation through iCalendar.

Domino 7 has centralized the processing of Rooms and Resources reservations into a new Rooms and Resources Manager (RNRMgr) task. This task is designed to prevent overbooking of rooms or resources, and is responsible for both the processing and the workflow that is related to reserving Rooms or a Resource, as well as accurately updating the Busytime database. (Note that this task replaces functionality that was previously handled in multiple places such as the router, the template of the Rooms and Resources database, and the Schedule Manager.) You can rename a Resource by changing its name, Site, and (if the resource is of type "Other") its category.

Domino 7 also offers improvements with the Lightweight Third Party Authentication (LTPA) scheme. Domino 7 provides the ability for an administrator to configure the name that should appear in a LTPA token when a Domino server generates it. Setting up an alternate LTPA user name does not require a pure Domino environment.

LEI

In **Lotus Enterprise Integrator** (**LEI**) 7, failover support in the Domino cluster environment is provided, so that if one server in a given implementation fails, activities continue processing on secondary, or subsequent, servers. The LEI Administrator incorporates new functionality, such as Sametime presence awareness and form-based connection testing.

LEI 7 includes the ability to control how dependent activities are run, based on the results of the calling activity. And you can have Data Management activities that use Notes connections to run under different Notes IDs.

Domino remote script debugging will now be able to debug the scripts used in Scripted Activities. Scripted Activities now record the connections used by the scripts, providing improved serviceability.

LEI, DECS, and the LSXLC are now fully integrated into Domino's NSD services. LEI scheduling dexterity is now improved, with better handling when you need to "Restrict to Schedule". LEI connection documents let you directly test your connections for validity. And virtual documents now properly handle back-end update and deletion synchronization.

Summary

This concludes our brief tour of new Notes 7 and Domino 7 functionality. For more complete information about these and all other new Notes 7 client and Domino 7 server features, see the book, *Upgrading to Lotus Notes and Domino 7*.

3

Lotus Notes/Domino 7 and DB2

For years, Lotus Domino has provided flexible data storage using "self-describing" documents. This has allowed developers to add and remove fields from document types on the fly. Each document stored within a Domino database contains a list of fields and their values.

Domino Designer combines visual form design with a data definition tool that allows you to update the fields stored within a document type throughout the lifetime of the application. This often tempts developers to create tables of fields within a form. In a relational word this may seem sacrilege, but in Notes/Domino development, this is more often than not considered acceptable.

Domino 7 DB2 integration is a new feature (currently offered via "Limited Availability"; see the note below) that provides the opportunity to close the gap between document-centric Notes/Domino and relational, SQL-based DB2. It allows you to bring the scalability features of DB2 and the flexibility of SQL into Domino applications. This feature encapsulates the storage facility from both end users and APIs.

In this chapter, we examine how to configure Domino 7 to use DB2 as an alternative data store to the NSF format. We also look at two important concepts in Domino/DB2 integration:

- **DB2 Access Views (DAVs)**, where selected data sets are pushed from Domino to DB2 in conjunction with a DB2 Access Server.

- **Query Views**, which are Notes views based on a SQL query. This design artifact is supported by the DB2 Access Server and a DB2 Access View.

The first release of Domino 7 and DB2 Integration is provided by IBM, solely for evaluation and testing purposes, with Limited Availability. It is currently unsupported. Further details can be found at http://www.lotus.com/ldd/d7db2.nsf. Full support for this feature will be provided in a later release. Consult the Notes/Domino 7 Release Notes to review the latest status.

DB2 as a Domino Data Store

When planning a DB2-based Domino application, remember that end users do not need their own DB2 connectivity. The Domino server fulfills this responsibility.

Creating a DB2-hosted Domino database results in a small NSF file that is created on the file system of the Domino server in its data directory. This file is typically smaller than a megabyte (often only a few kilobytes). DB2-backed Domino servers can replicate and cluster with traditional NSF-based Domino servers, so that both environments can co-exist if necessary. This can be particularly useful when testing Domino DB2 integration with existing Domino data.

The Domino and DB2 servers have the following possible relationships:

- The DB2 UDB server is installed locally on the Domino server.
- The DB2 UDB server is installed on a remote host accessible to the Domino server.

Testing environments typically leverage a DB2 UDB server that is installed locally on the machine where Domino is installed. The obvious advantage of this is local connectivity to the DB2 data store.

A number of Domino system databases are not supported for hosting by DB2. These include LOG.NSF, NAMES.NSF, DIRCAT.NSF, ADMIN4.NSF, DDM.NSF, and RESRC7.NSF (Rooms and Resources).

Prerequisites

Before you can install and configure DB2 as a Domino data store, there are several considerations you must address.

Software Required for the Domino Server

The Domino server must run Domino 7 or later. You must also install either the DB2 UDB server locally, or a DB2 Run-Time client, to catalog the DB2 "DOMINO" database. For remote installations where the DB2 server does not reside on the same host as the Domino server, one of the following must be installed locally on the machine where the Domino server executes in order for it to communicate with the DB2 host:

- DB2 Run-Time client

- DB2 UDB Enterprise Server Edition

- DB2 Workgroup Edition

Domino 7 and DB2 are available for these operating-system platforms:

- Microsoft Windows

- IBM AIX 5.2 and 5.3

Transactional Logging

The Domino server that will store its data in DB2 must have **transactional logging** enabled prior to installing DB2. To enable transaction logging, edit the Domino Server document belonging to the Domino server that will use DB2-based storage. Select the **Transactional Logging** tab and set the **Transactional logging** option to **Enabled**. Next, allocate at least **192 MB** in the **Maximum log space** field:

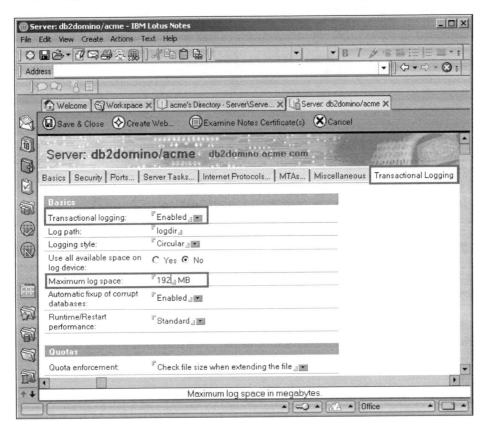

 The preceding screen shot depicts a **Circular Logging style**. Circular, Archived, or Linear styles are all allowed for this setting.

After **transactional logging** has been enabled, restart the Domino server. Domino will create the requested storage for the new transaction logs upon restart. You should see a message similar to the following, indicating that the requested logs are being created:

DB2 Installation Accounts

A DB2 installation account is necessary to install the DB2 software. Create this account and use it to log in to a local computer to install DB2. This user account is also used by the DB2 Server Enablement tool. This account can be either a local or domain user account created via either Windows or AIX. It must be a member of the Administrators group in use by the computer on which the DB2 software is to be installed. The account must also have the following privileges:

- Act as part of the operating system
- Create a token object
- Log in as a service
- Increase quotas
- Replace a process level token

When you're ready to install the DB2 software, use this account to log in to the target machine. Start the setup program, which includes important information detailing DB2 installation prerequisites. There is also a link to begin the product installation. Click it when all installation requirements have been met.

Installation and Configuration

This section examines an installation where the DB2 server is installed on the same machine as Domino.

The **Setup wizard** first prompts for an installation type. For DB2/Domino integration, you can select a **Typical** installation; **Data warehousing** and **Satellite administration capability** are not needed:

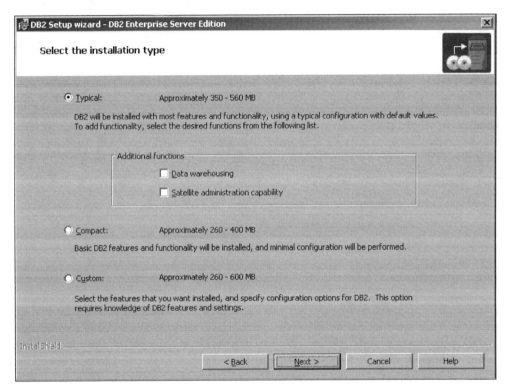

As the install program completes its work, it starts the DB2 software and displays a **First Steps** dialog. This dialog provides a link to create the sample database, which provides a convenient testing mechanism to verify connectivity to the DB2 server and the ability to catalog its databases. To create the sample database, click the **Create Sample Database** link located at the top left of the **First Steps** dialog. This displays the **Create Sample Databases** dialog. Confirm that the **DB2 UDB sample** option is checked, and then click **OK**.

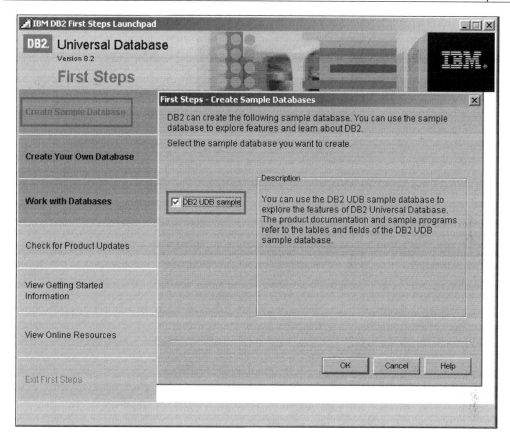

It can take several minutes to create the sample database. If successful, a message will confirm that the sample database was created.

Testing Connectivity to the DB2 Instance

The DB2 Server Enablement tool will fail if it cannot connect to the DB2 instance hosting the DOMINO database. We recommend that you test connectivity from the Domino host to the DB2 instance prior to enabling DB2 Domino storage. To do so, you must first determine which port the DB2 instance hosting the DOMINO database binds to. If you don't have this information, you can determine it by launching the DB2 Control Center: right-click on the **Server**, and select the **Export Server Profile** option from the **Context** menu.

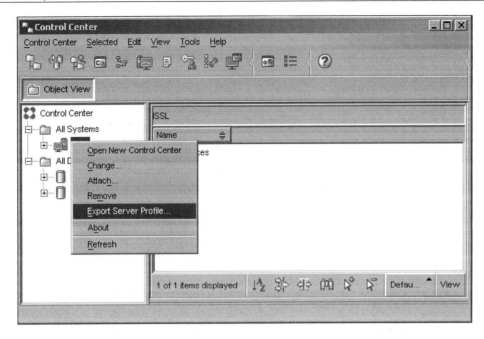

Selecting **Export Server Profile** prompts you for a destination filename. If successful, the **Control Center** responds by displaying the following dialog box:

After you export the file, open it and locate a section titled [inst>Instance Name], where Instance Name is the name of DB2 instance hosting the DOMINO database. Be sure that the Instance Name matches; many DB2 deployments have more than one instance deployed. After you find a match, locate the entry for **PortNumber**.

This entry appears in bold in the following output (in this example, the instance is located at port **50000**):

[inst>DB2]

NodeType=4

NodeNumber=0

DB2Comm=TCPIP

Authentication=SERVER

HostName=db2domino.acme.com

ServiceName=db2c_DB2

PortNumber=50000

IpAddress=192.168.1.104

QuietMode=No

SPMName=ISSL

TMDatabase=1ST_CONN

If you have uninstalled and reinstalled any versions of the DB2 software, then your DB2 instance may not communicate via port 50000. Instead, DB2 may increment to a higher port number, such as 50001. Verifying the contents of the **PortNumber** variable in the Domino DB2 instance increases the likelihood that the connectivity test succeeds.

Verifying DB2 Version Information

In some cases, it may be necessary to verify the version of DB2 installed to ensure it meets the requirements of Domino. To verify the version information of your DB2 software, open a DB2 Command Line Processor window and enter the db2level command:

```
C:\DB2 CLP                                                    _ □ ×
C:\Program Files\IBM\SQLLIB\BIN>db2level
DB21085I  Instance "DB2" uses "32" bits and DB2 code release "SQL08020" with
level identifier "03010106".
Informational tokens are "DB2 v8.1.7.445", "s040812", "WR21342", and FixPak
"7".
Product is installed at "C:\PROGRA~1\IBM\SQLLIB".

C:\Program Files\IBM\SQLLIB\BIN>_
```

Additional DB2 Configuration

The SYSCTRL group name must be set within DB2. The Domino online help documentation describes how to do this using the Command Line Processor. It can also be done using the Control Center. This section examines this step using the Command Line Processor.

To update SYSCTRL_GROUP, open a Command Line Processor window. Review the current configuration by typing GET DBM CFG at the prompt. Verify that the value is not set by reviewing the results. Set this value if needed.

The following screen shot shows the DB2 instance in need of this configuration step:

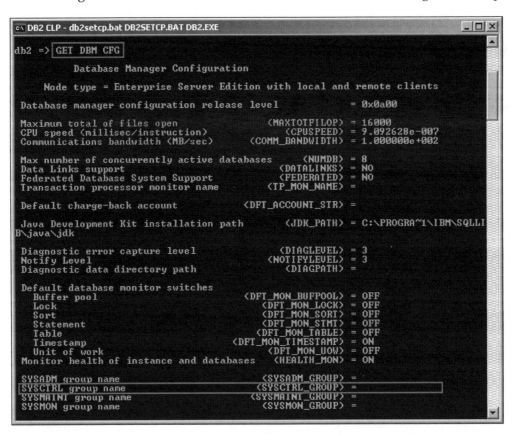

To set this value to DB2DOM, type the following into the Command Line Processor window:

UPDATE DBM CFG USING SYSCTRL_GROUP DB2DOM

After DB2DOM has been added to the SYSCTRL_GROUP, stop, and restart the DB2 instance using the DB2STOP and DB2START commands.

```
DB2 CLP - db2setcp.bat DB2SETCP.BAT DB2.EXE                    _□×
db2 => DB2STOP.
DB20000I  The DB2STOP command completed successfully.
db2 => DB2START
DB20000I  The DB2START command completed successfully.
db2 => _
```

The DB2 Server Enablement Tool

The DB2 Server Enablement tool configures Domino to use DB2 as its data store. The tool is available via the **Domino 7 Administrator** and is disabled by default. It resides in the **Configuration** tab, under **DB2 Server Tools** (you will notice the grayed-out tasks indicating that all **DB2 Server Tools** are disabled):

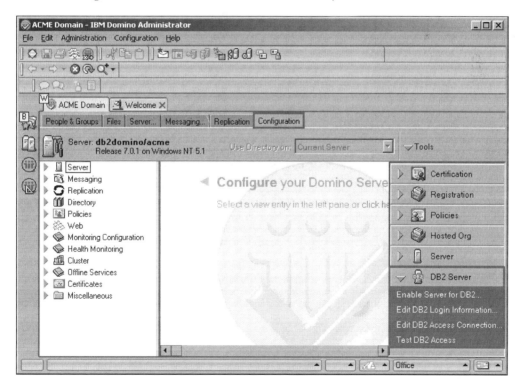

The DB2 Server Enablement tool requires that a DLL file be added to the Domino executable directory. In this example, the file is added to **C:\Lotus\Domino** as shown in the following figure:

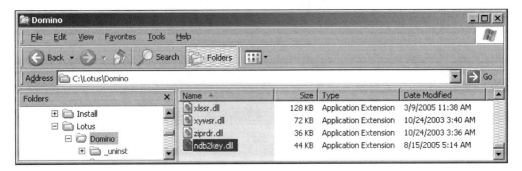

If this file is added to the executable directory while the Domino server is running, restart it as well as any **Domino Administrator** clients connected to it. Then verify that the **Enable Server for DB2...** tool has been enabled.

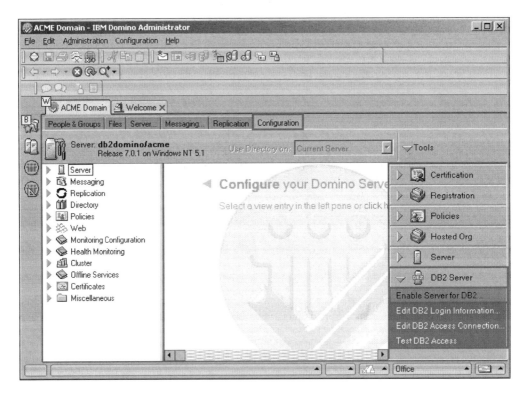

Click **Enable Server for DB2...** when you are ready to enable your DB2-based
Domino server. The following dialog box appears:

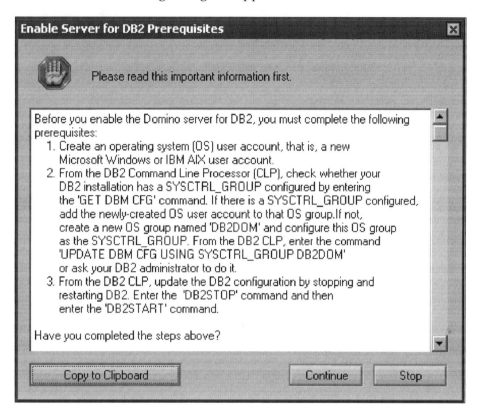

Verify that all requirements have been met, and then click **Continue**. The **Domino
7 Administrator** displays the **DB2 Server Enablement** tool. The **DB2 Server** tab of
the dialog prompts for information needed to create the **DB2 DOMINO** database.
Be sure that you have the name of the DB2 instance you intend to use for your DB2
DOMINO database. This value is specified in the **DB2 database name** field and defaults
to **DOMINO**. You can choose another name for the DB2 database the tool creates, if
needed. The **DB2 datastore directory** field is an optional field.

This dialog also allows you to specify whether the default Domino datastore for
new databases is NSF-based or DB2-based. There is an option to **Immediately
update the server's Domino Directory with DB2 information**, which when selected
causes the tool to process this update immediately. If deselected, update is later
processed by AdminP.

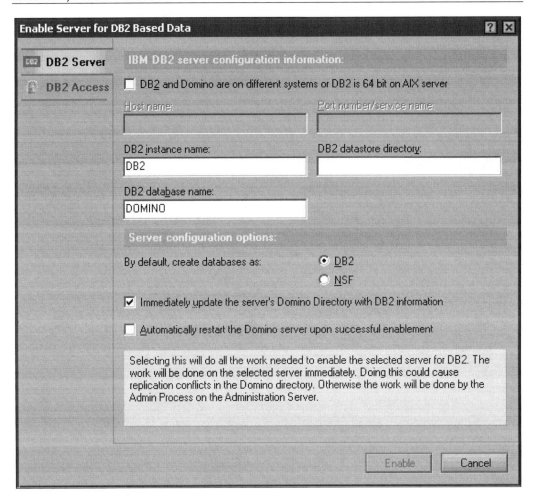

Next, click the **DB2 Access** tab and enter an **OS account name to be used by Domino to access DB2**. This dialog also requires the password associated with the OS account. After you enter this information, the **Enable** button is activated.

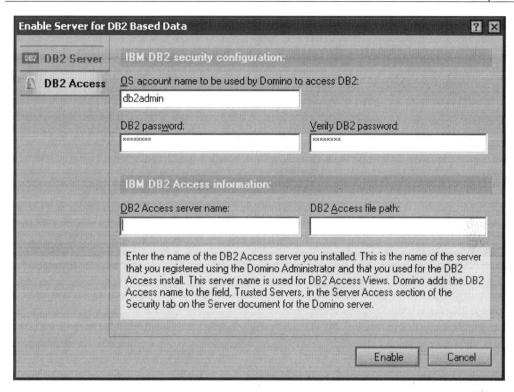

Clicking **Enable** displays the **Enable Server for DB2 Results** dialog, similar to the following figure:

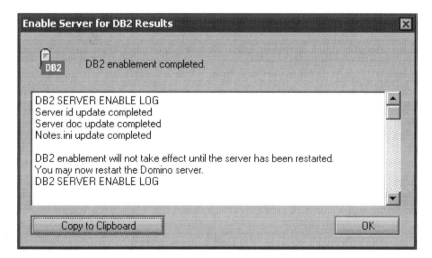

This step adds `notes.ini` variables to the server document. These variables are processed when the server restarts. Specifically, this step sets the `notes.ini` variable `DB2Init=Create` to direct the Domino server to create the requested DB2-based `DOMINO` database upon restart. If the Domino server successfully creates this database upon restart, it sets the `notes.ini` variable from `DB2Init=Create` to `DB2Init=OK`.

After the Domino server has been enabled for DB2 storage, the **DB2** tab appears in the DB2-enabled Domino server document as shown in the following figure:

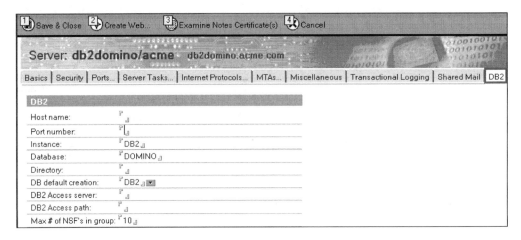

The field values should reflect those entered via the DB2 Server Enablement tool.

It is a good idea to open the DB2 **Control Center** and confirm that the **DOMINO** database was created on the **DB2** server. There are cases when the Domino server console may report that the database was created, when in fact it wasn't. You should see something similar to the screen shot that follows if the DB2 Domino data store was successfully created.

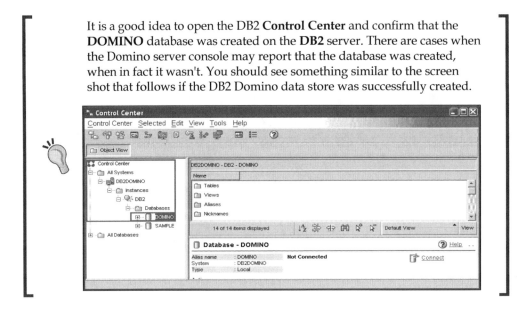

After the Domino server has been enabled for DB2 storage, you can take advantage of the benefits of using DB2 storage for new Domino databases. (Bear in mind that this does not convert existing Domino databases to DB2 storage.) At this point, you can optionally install the DB2 Access Server, which is necessary for creating DB2 Access Views and Query Views. These are discussed in the remainder of this chapter.

The DB2 Access Server, DB2 Access Views, and Query Views

The DB2 Access Server is an optional Domino 7 DB2 integration feature that governs access to Domino data when accessed from DB2. It is not required for DB2-based Domino storage, but DB2-based Domino storage is a requirement for the DB2 Access Server. The DB2 Access Server is, however, required for the use of DB2 Access Views and Query Views.

DB2 Access Views (DAVs) are Domino design artifacts that allow developers to push a set of Domino data into a DB2 view. Developers specify in each DAV a specific set of fields to be exported from Domino to DB2. The DB2 Access Server regulates access to the data stored in DAVs, using Domino security. Use of DAVs is not required for Domino to store data in DB2, but it is an optional extension of this integration that allows both Domino and DB2 clients to access this data.

Query Views are Domino design artifacts. They are similar to views but use SQL to populate their data sets. A Query View requires a DB2 Access View to construct its results. DB2 Access Views and Query Views both require a DB2 Access Server.

Installing the DB2 Access Server

Refer to the Domino 7 Release Notes prior to installing DB2 Access for Lotus Domino, for the latest information specific to your version of Domino. You can find the latest Release Notes by visiting www.lotus.com/ldd/notesua.nsf.

The first step in configuring a DB2 Access Server is to create a Domino server ID for it. To do so, open the **Domino Administrator** and click on the **Configuration** tab. Click **Registration | Server Task** in the **Tools** pane. This prompts the administrator to create the DB2 Access Server ID by either providing a Certifier ID or using the CA process if available.

The following procedure uses a Certifier ID. Open the **Basic** tab of the **Register New Server(s)** dialog, and do the following:

- Set the **ID file password** field to blank when registering a Server ID for a DB2 Access Server.
- Deselect the option to store the server ID in the Domino directory.
- Specify a file path for the server ID. This file will be needed by the DB2 Access Server software.

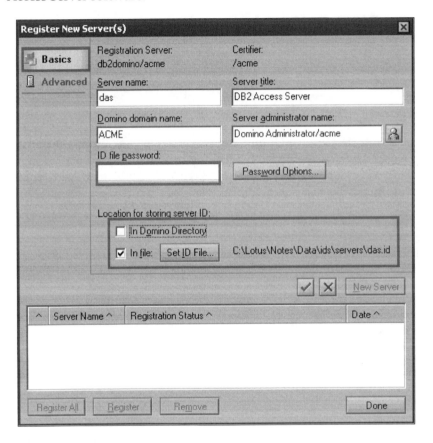

The **Advanced** tab of the **Register New Server(s)** dialog contains a new setting for DB2 Access Server IDs. When registering this server, enable the setting **This server is a DB2 Access server only**.

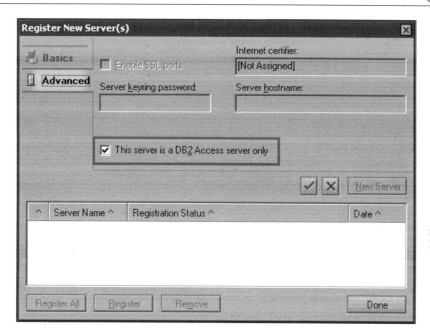

Click the **green checkmark** to add the DB2 Access Server to the registration queue. When you are ready, click **Register** or **Register All** to register your server. You are now ready to install the DB2 Access for Lotus Domino software.

> The DB2 Access for Lotus Domino software is installed on the DB2 server. This can be the same machine hosting the Domino server in a local DB2 configuration, but is not in remote DB2 configurations. At the time of writing, the DB2 Access for Lotus Domino software is available for download at www.software.ibm.com/webapp/ iwm/web/preLogin.do?source=ESD-BETA19.

Ensure that the DB2 Access Server's ID is available on the DB2 server's file system prior to the DB2 Access Server software installation. When you are ready, launch the setup program to start the **InstallShield Wizard** for DB2 Access for Lotus Domino. Click **Next** on the splash screen, where you will be given the opportunity to specify where to install the DB2 Access for Lotus Domino software for the DB2 server. The default setting is C:\Program Files\IBM\SQLLIB\FUNCTION. Be sure that this setting matches your DB2 server's FUNCTION directory.

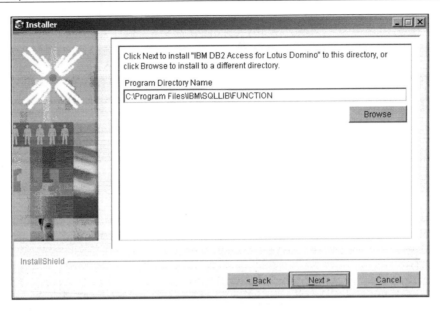

You are then prompted to specify the location of the ID file for the DB2 Access Server. Be sure that this directory is accessible by the DB2 server. If the DB2 server is not on the same machine as the Domino Administrator client that registered the server ID, it may have to be copied to the DB2 server host.

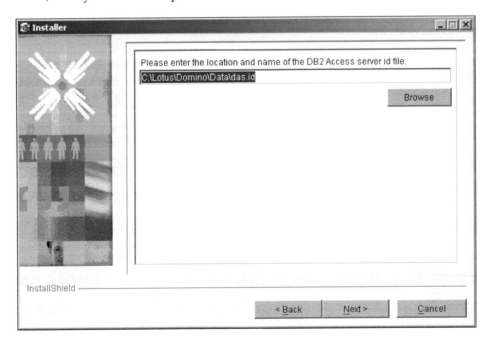

The **InstallShield** will then echo your installation selections back to you. Click **Next** if you are ready to install the product. When **InstallShield** has finished, it displays a dialog box indicating whether it was successful.

This completes the installation of the DB2 Access for Lotus Domino server software. When you are ready to enable the DB2 Access Server, proceed to the Domino server console and enter DB2 ACCESS SET as shown in the following figure.

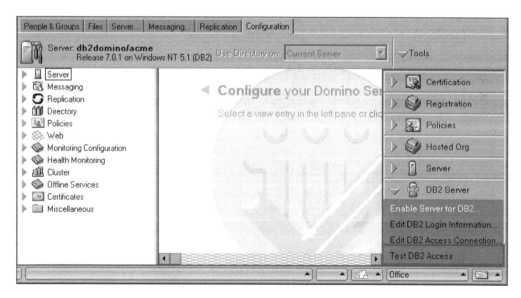

When this process completes, restart the Domino and DB2 servers. You can now test the DB2 Access Server using the **Domino Administrator**. To do so, open the **DB2 Server** tools and select **Test DB2 Access**.

You should see a dialog similar to the following, if you have set up your DB2 Access Server correctly.

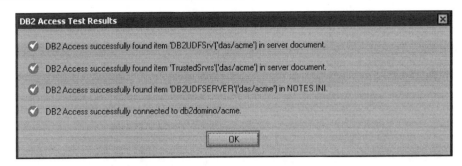

Congratulations! You have installed and configured the DB2 Access Server. You are now ready to create DB2 Access Views and Query Views.

DB2 Access Views

DB2 Access Views provide a means of pushing out a set of field data from Domino to a DB2 view. After the data arrives in the DB2 view, both Domino and DB2 clients can work with it in a manner consistent with Domino security. DB2 clients can also leverage their tool sets to take advantage of working with the data directly in relational format. The DB2 Access Server governs security. (Remember that it must be installed prior to creating DB2 Access Views.)

Creating the DB2 Access View Definition

DB2 Access Views are created via **Domino Designer 7**. To create one, select **Shared Resources | DB2 Access Views**, and click **New DB2 Access View**.

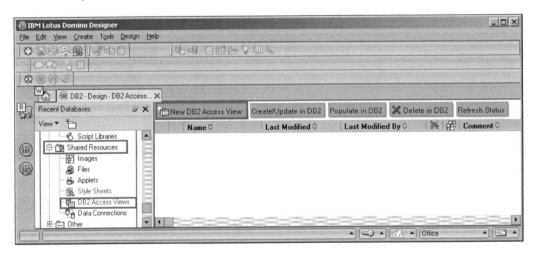

This opens the **DB2 Access View Designer**. You will need to assign a name to your DB2 Access View. This name becomes the name of the DB2 view when it is later created there.

The **DB2 Access View**'s infobox provides several options worth reviewing. There is an option to select which forms' data to include in the DB2 Access View. You can select all forms, or select them individually. There is also an option, **Compute with form on DB2 insert or update**, which can be applied to inserts or updates that occur to the data via DB2, as well as an option to specify a **Default form to use for DB2 inserts** in cases where the form field is not set. Setting a default form value ensures that the data displays using the correct form when viewed via a Notes client.

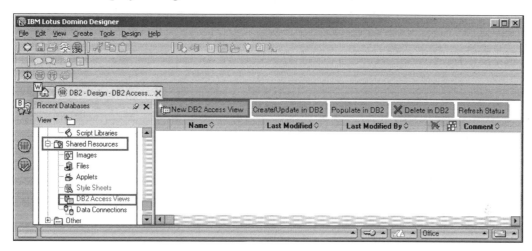

The **DB2 Access View Designer** is visually similar to the Outline Designer. You create entries using buttons located at the top of the Designer. Use the **Choose Field** button to select a field from the Notes database. Use the **Insert Field** button to manually define data for the DB2 View that is created as a result of this process.

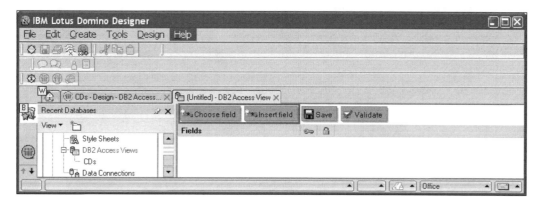

Selecting **Choose Field** displays a dialog box that allows you to select fields from a list defined for the current database. Fields can be selected from throughout the database, or the list can be filtered to enumerate field definitions based on form, subform, or shared field definitions. The fields selected in this dialog box define the set of data to be pushed into the corresponding DB2 view.

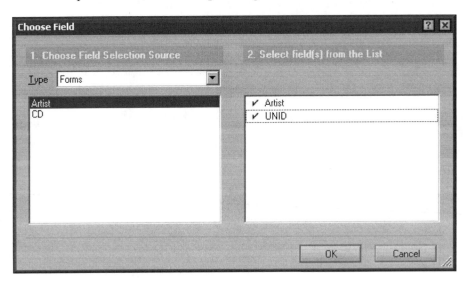

After you have specified the set of field data to be published to the DB2 view, click **OK**. This adds the set of selected fields to the **DB2 Access View Outline**.

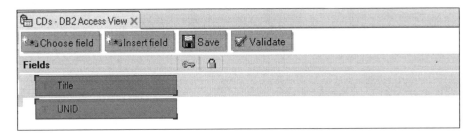

 It may seem tempting to export all of your data using a single DB2 Access View. This puts most data at your fingertips but may make queries against your data more complicated. Defining concise data sets for your DB2 Access View simplifies querying it for data, and allows for greater flexibility when joining it with other data sets.

When you are satisfied with the fields selected in your outline, click **Save**, and close the **DB2 Access View Designer**. This returns you to the list of DB2 Access View design elements.

The next step is to propagate your DB2 Access View definition from Domino Designer to the DB2 server. To do this, close the **DB2 Access View Designer** so that you are returned to the **DB2 Access View** design view. Select the **DB2 Access View** you created, and click the **Create/Update in DB2** action button.

If this action is successful, you should see a dialog box similar to the following, indicating that the Access Definition was created:

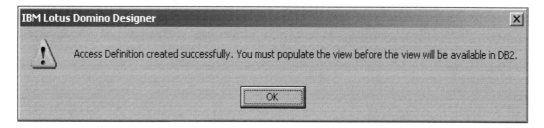

Populating DB2 with Domino Data

So far, we have only created the DB2 Access View definition. The next step is to populate DB2 with Domino data. To do so, select the **DB2 Access View** in the design view, and click the **Populate in DB2** button.

Clicking this button initiates a request for the Domino server to populate the DB2 view with data. You should see a dialog box similar to the following:

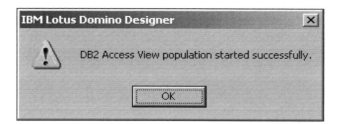

This is an asynchronous process; large data sets could take some time to populate. If the DB2 Access Server is correctly configured, the Domino server console should send messages similar to those appearing in the next illustration, indicating the status of the operation.

```
db2domino/acme: Lotus Domino Server                              _ □ ×
08/09/2006  01:25:46 PM  DAVPOP: Started
08/09/2006  01:25:46 PM  DAVPOP: Populating DAV: CDs_By_Artist
08/09/2006  01:25:47 PM  DAVPOP: Shutdown
08/09/2006  01:27:22 PM  Opened session for das/acme (Release 7.0.1)
08/09/2006  01:27:46 PM  Opened session for das/acme (Release 7.0.1)
>
```

The DB2 Access View is fully populated after the DAVPOP task confirms its shutdown.

Mapping DB2 User Names to Domino

The DB2 Access View has now been populated with data. If you intend to access Domino data in the DB2 Access View using a DB2 client, you should map Domino to DB2 names using the Domino Administrator's **DB2** tools. If you do not map DB2 user names to Domino Person documents, the DB2 Access Server will request access to Domino data for DB2 users as Anonymous.

To map a DB2 user to a Domino Person document, open the **Domino 7 Administrator**, and click the **People & Groups** tool. Select the **Person** document belonging to the ID that you want to use to access Domino data in DB2. If you plan to populate the DB2 user name with the Domino shortname field, verify that this field has been populated prior to launching the **Set DB2 User Name...** tool. You can edit the selected **Person** document directly within the **Domino Administrator** if necessary. When ready, click the **Set DB2 User Name...** tool.

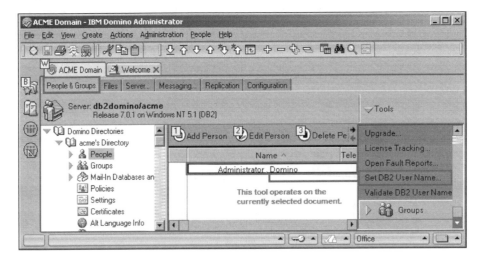

This launches the **Set DB2 User Name** dialog:

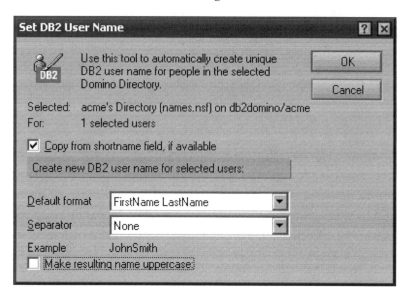

If you plan to populate the DB2 user name field using the Domino shortname field, check **Copy from shortname field, if available**. Also check **Make resulting name uppercase**, if needed.

Click **OK** when you have populated the requested input fields. This instructs the **Set DB2 User Name** tool to populate the selected **Person** document with a DB2 ID that maps the user to a Domino name. This allows the DB2 Access Server to enforce Domino security for users accessing Domino data via a DB2 client. If this operation is successful, you should see a message similar to the following:

DB2 user names must be unique. If you have a large directory, you may need to run the **Validate DB2 User Names...** tool from the **Domino Administrator**. When running this tool, the **Domino Administrator** prompts the user to select the scope of validation.

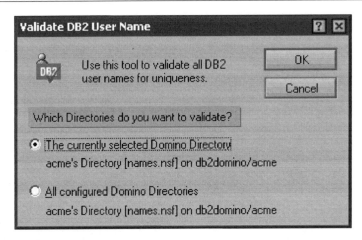

Select **The currently selected Domino Directory** option if your DB2 use of Domino data is limited to the primary Domino directory. Select **All configured Domino Directories** if DB2 client use of Domino data occurs via users in secondary Domino directories.

You can verify the results of this tool by viewing the **Person** document. Open it to the **Administration** tab, and verify that the **DB2 account name** field was updated as requested.

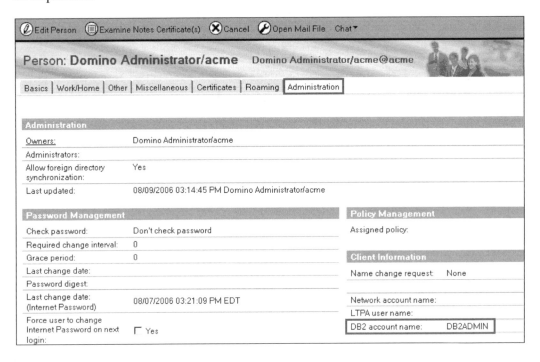

In the preceding example, the DB2 user **DB2ADMIN** is mapped to the Domino user **Domino Administrator/acme** when accessing data from a DB2 client. To test accessing your Domino data from DB2, open the DOMINO database in **DB2**. Select **Views**, and locate the name of the DB2 Access View. If spaces occur in the name of the DB2 Access View, they are replaced with underscores. In the following illustration, a DB2 user selects the **CDS** DB2 Access View via the **Control Center**.

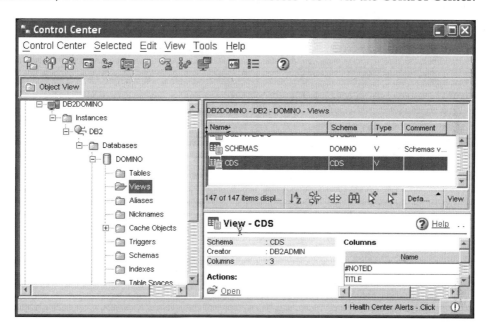

Double-click **View** to open it. You should see your Domino data as hosted by DB2.

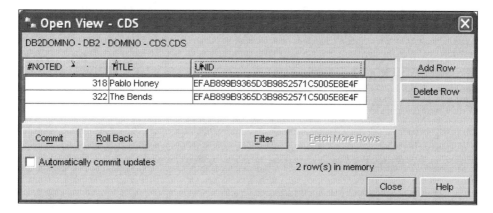

Congratulations! You have created a DB2 Access View and can now access its data from a DB2 client. This allows you to aggregate the DB2 tool set with your Domino data, providing the power and flexibility of SQL along with it. The last design artifact we will look at is the Query View.

Query Views

Query Views allow you to leverage the data stored in DB2 Access Views within a Domino view using SQL. Query Views require a DB2 Access View to function.

Query Views are created in the same manner as standard Domino views. Open **Domino Designer**, and select **Views**. Then click the **Create View** action. When the DB2 Access Server is enabled, a new radio button option appears for **Selection conditions**, labeled **By SQL Query**. Select this radio button to create a **Query View**. Your SQL must also be enclosed in quotes, or **Domino Designer** will process your SQL as an @Formula:

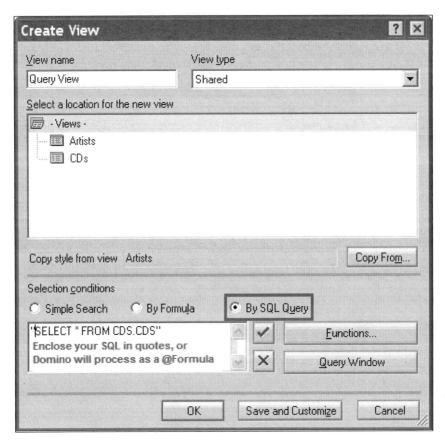

When you click **OK**, the **View Designer** appears. Query Views contain an additional object labeled **SQL Query**. Select this to update the SQL your view consists of. Your view can inherit a standard Domino view selection formula if your view was copied from another. Verify that the view selection formula does not contain additional selection criteria that alter the results of your SQL query. If necessary, remove the contents of the View Selection object so that only the SQL query governs the result set. The SQL query object is highlighted in the following:

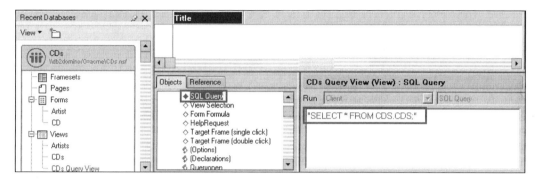

After you have finished defining your view, **Save** and close it. Query Views cannot be previewed in Notes. To verify the result set, open the **Query View** in the Notes client, where you should see your data. Notice that **Query Views** identify themselves using a different icon from standard Domino views.

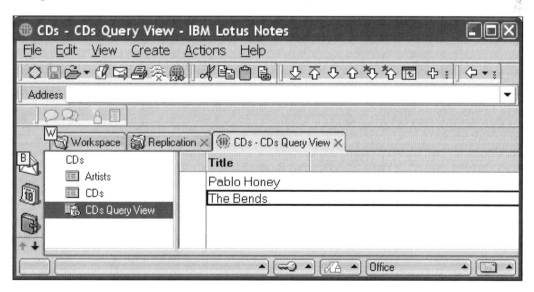

Query Views do not store their data in Domino in the same manner that a Domino view caches its data. Query Views are Domino views of data stored in DB2 that are constructed dynamically. Query Views also provide the capability to join data from multiple data sets stored in DB2. This lets you join data from multiple Domino databases, if those databases have all exported their data to a DB2 Access View.

Summary

In this chapter, we studied how to use DB2 as a data store for Domino databases. We reviewed the installation and configuration procedures for DB2-based Domino storage. We then looked at how to export Domino data to a DB2 View using DB2 Access Views. We identified the process for mapping DB2 user IDs to Domino user IDs. We then went on to look at accessing Domino data from a DB2 client. Finally, we examined how to work with Domino data using relational design constructs using SQL-based Query Views. At this point, you are ready to leverage the power of DB2 and Domino!

4

New Lotus Domino Designer
7 Features

Lotus Domino Designer 7 offers new features designed to help you better manage Lotus Notes and Domino applications, provide new user-interface elements, and provide better support for newer technologies such as Web Services.

In this chapter, we examine these new features and explain how you can get more out of Domino Designer 7. Major features include:

- AutoSave
- Design enhancements, including shared columns, Design view features, input enabled formulas, default form indicator, design elements improvements, and new SmartIcons
- Agent profiling
- Java enhancements, including Sun Java support and remote Java debugging

These and other features are discussed in the following sections.

AutoSave

Domino Designer 7 includes a new AutoSave feature. This allows you to automatically backup any documents open in Edit mode to a defined AutoSave database. If the editing session is interrupted before you can save the document, you can retrieve the version of the document residing in the AutoSave database and restore your edits. AutoSave also allows you to backup, on demand, any documents currently open in Edit mode into the AutoSave database.

AutoSave databases are defined on a per-user basis. This prevents the sharing of documents backed up into the AutoSave database by multiple user IDs.

Configuring the Lotus Notes Client for AutoSave

Although AutoSave is generally considered a Domino Designer enhancement (also see Chapter 5), there is also an administrative component involved. Each Lotus Notes 7 client that uses this feature must enable it in the **User Preferences** dialog. To do so, select **File | Preferences | User Preferences** from the Notes client, and enable the **AutoSave every** check box:

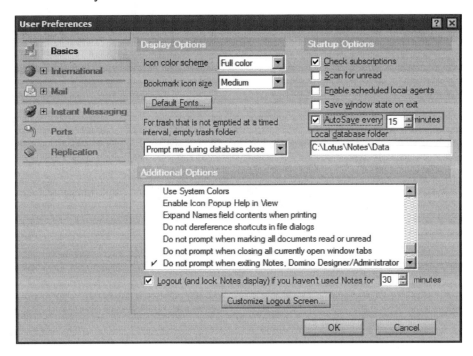

AutoSave runs at a scheduled interval. (In the preceding example, this is set to 15 minutes.) It can also be initiated manually by selecting **File | AutoSave | AutoSave Now**. The default value is 15 minutes, but this can be adjusted as required. Note that, when enabling AutoSave for the first time, Notes responds with the following dialog box, indicating that AutoSave will not be enabled until after the Notes client is restarted.

In most cases, the AutoSave database is created automatically when the Notes 7 client is first installed. In some instances, the AutoSave database must be created manually. If necessary, create the AutoSave database by following these steps:

1. From the Notes client, select **File | Database | New**.

2. Select **Show Advanced Templates** in the **New Database** dialog.

3. Select **Autosave** from the **Template** list. (This entry will not appear unless **Show Advanced Templates** is selected.)

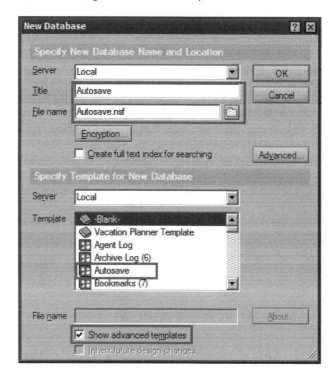

4. Enter **Autosave.nsf** in the **File name** field.

5. Click **OK**.

The AutoSave database does not contain any forms. It contains one view, **$AutoSave**, that identifies the server, database, and document that is saved into it:

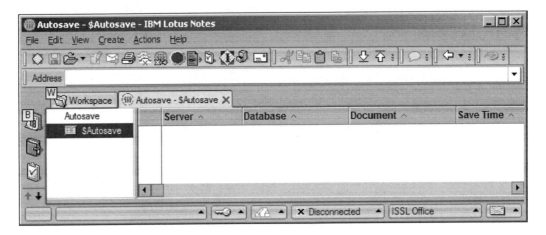

The name of the Autosave database is specified on a per-user basis by setting the notes.ini variable, AUTO_SAVE_USER, for each user using AutoSave on that Notes client installation. For example, the following notes.ini entry sets an AutoSave database filename as_SCooke.nsf for user Stephen Cooke/Acme:

```
AUTO_SAVE_USER,Stephen Cooke/Acme=as_SCooke.nsf
```

If your AutoSave requirements include user-level security, consider adding additional AUTO_SAVE_USER entries using a similar format that specify a different database for each user. When doing so, be sure to configure the ACLs of each AutoSave database so that access to each is restricted to their respective owners.

Configuring Applications for AutoSave

After the Notes 7 client is configured for AutoSave support, individual applications must also be configured to use this feature. AutoSave is enabled within applications on a form-by-form basis. To enable a form to support AutoSave:

1. Open the form design dialog in Domino Designer 7.

2. Open the form properties infobox.

3. Place a checkmark next to **Allow AutoSave** in the **Options** section of the Form Information tabbed page.

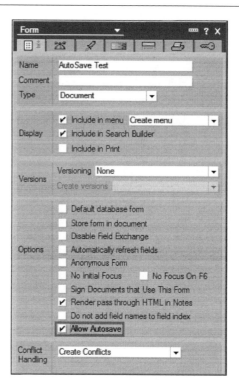

Repeat this process for each form requiring AutoSave support.

The Notes client's Status Bar logs AutoSave events. When the editing session for a document exceeds the AutoSave interval, the Status Bar logs messages indicating AutoSave activity:

The preceding Status Bar messages indicate that a document open for editing has been successfully AutoSaved. If the Notes 7 client is shut down abnormally and the AutoSave database contains documents when Notes is next launched, AutoSave presents the user with the following dialog box:

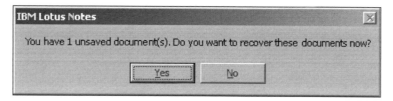

If you select **Yes**, Notes 7 displays a list of AutoSaved documents available for recovery:

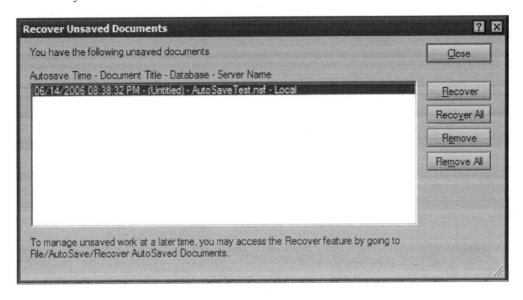

To continue editing an AutoSaved document, select it and click the **Recover** button. This will restore the selected document in Edit mode.

Do not assume that all applications will support AutoSave in the same manner. Some form designs use global variables that may not be restored correctly during AutoSave restoration. Each form intended for use with AutoSave should be tested to determine its compatibility with the feature. Also bear in mind that the AutoSave interval is configured globally for the Notes 7 client. It can not be changed on an application-by-application basis.

Design Enhancements

Lotus Domino Designer 7 offers a number of new design features. These include shared columns, input-enabled formulas, Default Form indicator, design element improvements, and new SmartIcons.

Shared Columns

Shared columns provide a mechanism for reusing a view column definition across multiple views. This helps ensure UI consistency across your application. To create a shared column, open the database in Domino Designer 7, and select **Shared Code | Columns** from the design navigator:

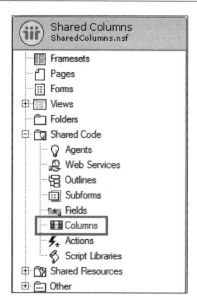

Each time a shared column is saved, Domino Designer displays the following dialog box:

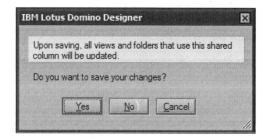

This warning reminds you that all views and folders that use the shared column will also be updated. Be aware that updating a shared column in this manner causes Domino Designer to resave and sign any view that includes the shared column using the current user ID. Designers unfamiliar with the entire application might not know which views use the shared column, and hence may be hesitant to update it. To address this problem, the shared column Design view provides a view action to identify any view that uses the selected shared column via a button labeled **Who is using this Shared Column**:

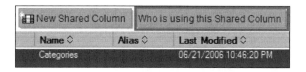

Clicking this button displays a dialog box that identifies all views using this shared column, for example:

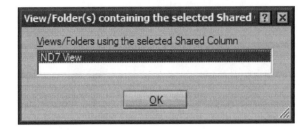

A shared column can be inserted into a view while it is open in Domino Designer. Use the **Create** menu option to do this:

This brings up a dialog containing a list of all the shared columns in the database:

Choose the shared column to be included in the view, and click the **Insert** button. (The dialog displays an **Insert** button when either inserting or appending a new shared column.)

A shared column allows you to specify both formulas and formatting. In some cases, you may want to define only the formulas contained within the shared-column design, and allow other developers who are using it to apply their own formatting options. This option is governed by the developer who is using the shared column, not the ones designing it. To override the formatting options provided by the shared column, select **Use Formula Only** in the **Insert Shared Column** dialog:

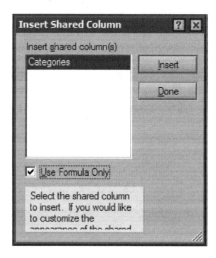

This option ensures consistent formula design, and also allows the shared column to fit in visually with the view hosting it.

Design View

Domino Designer 7 updates the Design view by retaining column widths set in the Design view for any given database. This setting is retained on a database-by-database basis. When you set the column width of a Design view within a given database, Designer maintains the same column widths for Design views of all design note categories within that database. This applies to all Design Views. The following illustration is an example of a column width retained within a given database:

Input-Enabled Formulas

Input-enabled formulas allow you to define whether or not a field is editable using a @formula that evaluates to @True or @False. The Domino Designer 7 documentation indicates that this feature is available only to "Native OS" style fields, but we have found that this feature is also available to Notes style fields.

Input-enabled formulas are configured via the Objects field navigator for the selected field. A formula that evaluates to @True allows the field to be edited. A formula that evaluates to @False prevents that field from being edited. The following input-enabled formula prevents the selected field from being edited in documents with a Subject field value of Test.

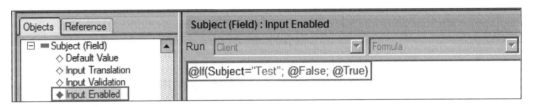

The Default Form Indicator

Domino Designer 7 has updated the Default Form indicator. When a form has its "Default database form" property set, it displays a graphical image of a star next to the form. Only one form at a time can have this property set. Setting this attribute for one form disables it for all others.

Design Elements

Lotus Domino Designer 7 includes two enhancements that improve the handling of design elements.

Design Elements Sortable by Name

Domino Designer 6 did not allow you to sort design elements using the Name column in the Design Elements view, although it did allow design elements to be sorted by other columns. In Domino Designer 7, design elements are now sortable by the Name field.

Inline Editing of Design Elements

Domino Designer 7 allows you to edit the attributes that appear in the Design view of various design elements, without the need to open the design notes. This can now be done inline from the Design Elements view. Simply click on the design note and attribute in the Design Elements view, and an edit field appears, allowing you to make immediate changes:

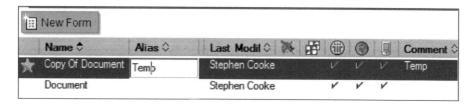

New SmartIcons

Domino Designer 7 provides several new SmartIcons. Perhaps the most useful of them is **Debug LotusScript**, shown in the following:

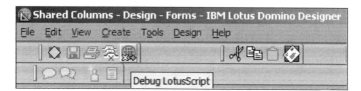

Coupled with this new SmartIcon, Lotus Notes 7 and Domino Designer 7 no longer display a modal dialog box indicating the new state of the debugger. In place of the modal dialog box, a message is sent to the status bar indicating the new state of the debugger. In the following screenshot, the debugger has indicated that the most recent click of the Debug LotusScript SmartIcon has placed the debugger into an active state:

This SmartIcon is a toggle button; clicking it a second time restores it to its original state.

A second SmartIcon of interest, labeled **Close All Open Window Tabs**, has been added to the Universal toolbar. It appears in both the Domino Designer 7 and Lotus Notes 7 clients.

Clicking the toolbar button in the following screenshot closes all open window tabs:

This SmartIcon corresponds to the **File | Close All Open Window Tabs** that has been added to both the Lotus Notes 7 and Domino Designer 7 menus:

Agent Profiling

Agent profiling allows developers and administrators to collect performance data for a LotusScript or Java-based agent. When programming Java-based agents, this feature is only available for Java agents edited directly within the Domino 7 Designer, not Imported Java classes.

Profiling is enabled through the Agent Properties infobox:

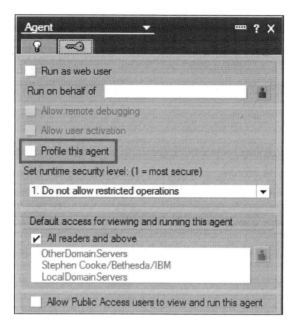

Agent profiling collects performance data during each subsequent iteration of the agent. This applies to both local and server-based agents. When you select an agent design note containing profiling data in the Design view, a new menu item (**View Profile Results**) appears at the bottom of the **Agent** menu:

Selecting this option displays a Performance document, which details the performance of various calls from within the agent. The following information is detailed in the Performance document:

- Class indicates the object class of the object invoked.
- Method indicates the member method invoked from the object variable.

- Operation is Get or Set where appropriate. A Get operation reads data from the variable; a Set operation updates the in-memory copy of the variable.
- Calls identifies the number of times the method was called.
- Time is the amount of time elapsed during the call.

The following table contains sample performance data from a profiled agent:

Performance Profiling Sample Profile

07/12/2006 08:59:49 AM EDT
Elapsed time: 30 msec
Methods profiled: 6
Total measured time: 30 msec

Class	Method	Operation	Calls	Time
Document	[expandedname]	Set	1	30
Database	GetView		1	0
Document	Save		1	0
Session	CurrentDatabase	Get	1	0
View	GetFirstDocument		1	0
Document	[expandedname]	Get	1	0

Domino Designer 7 provides the LotusScript NotesAgent class with a new method, GetPerformanceDocument, which provides programmatic access to the Performance document. The method returns a NotesDocument object that can be opened into the workspace, emailed, and so on.

 Opening a Performance document via Domino Designer UI at least once prior to accessing it programmatically often produces better results.

Profiling is also available for Web Services, a new design element available in Domino Designer 7. Web Services are covered in detail in Chapter 8 of this book.

Accessing Modified Documents

Notes and Domino 7 support a new method of accessing a database's document collection based on specifying a date threshold. Any documents that have been updated since the specified threshold time are grouped via a document collection to the caller. It also provides a secondary argument that acts as a filter on the document collection returned. The method can return data documents, or various types of design elements based on the filter passed in the second argument.

Right Mouse Button

Domino Designer 7 now supports the creation of actions associated with the right mouse button. These are available for Shared Columns and View Actions, but not for Form Actions. The right mouse button provides a means of reducing the amount of screen required by the View Action bar. This setting appears in the infobox of Shared Actions and View Actions:

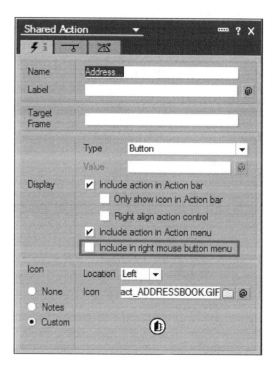

Java

Domino Designer 7 includes improved Java integration, including Sun Java support and remote Java debugging.

Sun Java Support

Notes and Domino 7 support the Sun Java™ 2 platform, Technology Edition v1.4.2. Care should be taken to run Java agents compiled on Domino 7 servers and Notes 7 clients. The standard Notes Java archives included with release 7 should not be used on Java platforms earlier than v1.4.2.

Remote Java Debugging

Notes and Domino Designer 7 now support remote Java debugging for Java code that runs in a Notes client JVM. IBM recommends that this be used only on an as-needed basis while troubleshooting, as debugging Java code degrades performance.

Java Debugging can occur within three contexts:

- **Foreground**, in which Java code is triggered interactively by the user. An example includes starting an agent using the menu.
- **Background**, in which Java code is run by a task loader. Locally scheduled agents are run in this manner.
- **Web Preview**, which includes Java code being previewed in a browser via Domino Designer. Applets loaded into forms fall under this category.

Each of the preceding contexts has its own JVM. Only one user at a time can debug in a given context. Several things must occur to support the remote debugging of a Java agent:

- The computer must use a Java debugger that supports the Java Platform Debugger Architecture. Eclipse is an open-source product that meets this criterion.
- Java Debugging preferences must be set via the **Java Debugging Preferences** menu item:

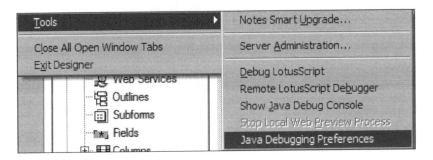

Selecting this menu item brings up the following dialog box:

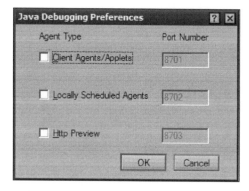

- Check **Client Agents/Applets** to enable foreground debugging. Use the **Port Number** field to specify a port to connect the Notes and debugger computers.

- Check **Locally Scheduled Agents** to debug background agents. This also requires a port specification to connect the Notes and debugger computers.

- Check **Http Preview** to debug Java run in Web Preview mode. This context also requires that a port be specified to connect the Notes and debugger computers.

The next step in debugging Java code remotely involves configuring the individual Java agent, Web Service, or script library to support it. To do so, open the design element, and on the **Security** tab, check the **Compile Java code with debugging information**.

The following steps are necessary to start your debugging session:

1. Connect a debugger to the JVM. The remainder of this procedure assumes you're using the Eclipse debugger.
2. Start the Notes client containing the agent or Web service to debug after Java debugging has been enabled.
3. Start the Eclipse debugger.
4. Create an Eclipse-based Java project. Open the Java perspective if it is not already open.
5. Import the Java source files into a Java project using the Import context menu in the Java perspective.
6. Start the Java agent or Web Service to be debugging in Notes 7 or Designer 7.

Attach the Eclipse-based debugger to the Notes JVM, and then choose **Run | Debug** from the menu. This opens a dialog box that manages launch configurations. Create a new Debug configuration. Click the **Connect** tab, and specify the Java project, the host name or IP address of the Notes computer, and the Java debug port specified in the Notes client. If both Notes/Designer 7 and Eclipse are on the same machine, you can enter 127.0.0.1 for the host-name field.

Suspending a thread allows you to apply full debugger control to code. This provides a means of setting breakpoints, step through code, and enumerate variables.

Debugging Java code over a network is not secure. Once you have finished troubleshooting an issue, disable debugging to increase performance and harden security.

Summary

This concludes our examination of new Domino Designer 7 features. We examined the AutoSave database, the use of shared columns and other enhancements to the Domino Designer 7 client, and remote Java debugging. Of course, there is much more to these features than can be covered in a single chapter. For in-depth details about these features and how to use them, consult the Lotus Domino Designer 7 product documentation.

5

Upgrading Domino Applications

This chapter takes a closer look at several new features in Lotus Notes 7 and Lotus Domino Designer 7 clients that raise specific upgrade issues. In this chapter, we will identify some of those new features, show you how to implement them, and what to watch out for or think about. For a complete description of all the new features in Domino Designer 7, see Chapter 4.

When upgrading applications, you should keep two goals in mind. The first is to ensure interoperability; that is making sure that your clients can use your applications at least as well after upgrading as before. The second goal is to identify the critical handful of features whose implementation will add enough sizzle or functionality to your application for your users to applaud the upgrade (and thus be motivated to ensure the upgraded applications are quickly accepted and adopted). For your users, this mitigates the nuisance of upgrading.

Notes/Domino 7 offers some tremendous back-end improvements over previous releases. On the user-visible front-end, the improvements are more incremental. This is good news in that your users won't need extensive retraining, but of course, it also narrows the field in terms of finding those sharp new features that will make them excited to upgrade.

To help you identify which features offer the most visible and immediate value to your users, we'll take a quick tour of several features that we feel offer the most "bang for the buck" from the perspective of an end-user. First, let's examine several high-profile Lotus Notes client features added in release 7.

Lotus Notes 7 Client Features

The following list describes several of the more user-visible features that have been added or enhanced in the Lotus Notes 7 client. These features can comprise a compelling reason for your users to upgrade:

- **AutoSave** saves your work without user intervention. For example, with AutoSave enabled, if your computer crashes, you will be able to reboot and recommence working at roughly the same point where you left off in any open documents.

- **Mail and the Resource & Reservations database** are enhanced but not radically changed. On the back-end, however, the Resource & Reservations database has been dramatically upgraded to better avoid scheduling conflicts.

- **Message Disclaimer**, a highly sought after feature, allows users and/or administrators to add a message disclaimer to every outgoing email. This is done through policy documents. The disclaimer is added after the user sends the outgoing email message, as opposed to a signature that the user sees before sending.

- **Save/Close all windows** lets you close all window tabs from the **File** menu (via the option **Close All Open Window Tabs**). You can also save the state of you open windows, either from the **File** menu (manually) or as a default setting under **User Preferences** (which makes it automatic). This means that when you reopen Notes, all these window tabs will be loaded for you. Note that it is only the tab window references that are loaded, not the actual views or documents. So when you click on one of these tabs, there may be a slight delay as the view is refreshed or the document is reloaded. The alternative would be that you would have to wait for all of these views and documents to be loaded just to get into Notes, which would be unreasonable.

Of the preceding features, AutoSave in particular is likely to be of interest to your users, so we will look at it in a bit more detail later in this chapter.

New Domino Designer Client Features

Some of the important and valuable new/upgraded features for the Domino Designer 7 include the following:

- **AutoSave** (mentioned above, and described in more detail later in this chapter).

- **Agent Profiler** allows a developer to see how long every call in their agent is taking, and how many times each of those calls occurs. This is an invaluable tool for performance monitoring and troubleshooting, and we'll look at it in more detail in Chapter 11, *Troubleshooting Applications*.

- **Domino Domain Monitoring (DDM)** is perhaps the single most important feature in Notes/Domino 7. It provides an extensive list of troubleshooting and performance monitoring tools, a subset of which is relevant for application developers. We will examine this in more detail in Chapter 11.

- **Significant improvements to referencing profile documents in views** have been made. In addition to changing the color scheme for a view, you can now develop applications that are much more user-defined and dynamic. This will be described in detail later in this chapter.

- **Right-clicks in views brings up the action bar buttons**. This is an incremental improvement, but in terms of overall usability in the product, it is a nice feature to have.

- **Shared view columns** allow a developer to create complex and widely used view columns and then apply the shared design to multiple views. Any changes to that shared column design will automatically be reflected in all the views that reference that column.

- **In-place design element editing of labels** is a very handy way for developers to change the names of forms, views, agents, and so on, without having to open and resave the design element. While highlighting a design element, you simply click to enter in-place editing, and you can use the *Tab* key to move along the row to edit different labels for the same design element. This feature works much the same as InViewEditing does for Notes clients.

- **Web Services** are described in a later section.

- **DB2 design integration** is also discussed in a separate section.

AutoSave

As mentioned previously, AutoSave allows you to automatically save your work periodically without having to do so manually. If your computer crashes, you'll be able to resume your work at the point AutoSave last ran. This helps avoid the situation where you lose hours of work because you forgot to save as you went along, which has probably happened to everyone at least once!

Two things have to happen to enable the AutoSave feature: the user has to turn on the setting, and the application developer must enable AutoSave for the form the user is currently working on. For users to enable AutoSave on their clients, they must select **File | Preferences | User Preferences**. On the **Basics** tab in the **Startup Options** section, there is a new setting **AutoSave every n minutes**, where **n** is the number of minutes between auto-saves. This interval can be from 1 to 999 minutes. (You must close and reopen Notes for AutoSave to be enabled.)

For the developer, AutoSave must be enabled on a form-by-form basis. Open the form in Domino Designer, and select **Design | Form Properties**. Then check the new option **Allow Autosave**.

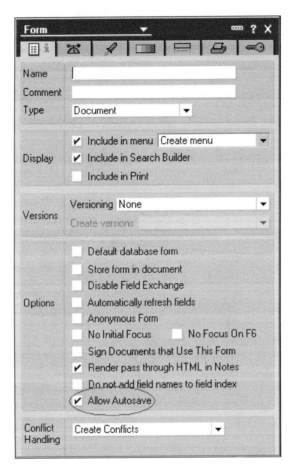

With AutoSave enabled, when you are working in a document with this form and experience a computer crash or power outage, you will see the following dialog box on restarting Notes:

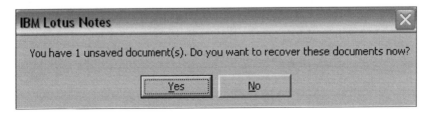

If you choose **Yes**, then you'll see a popup similar to the following:

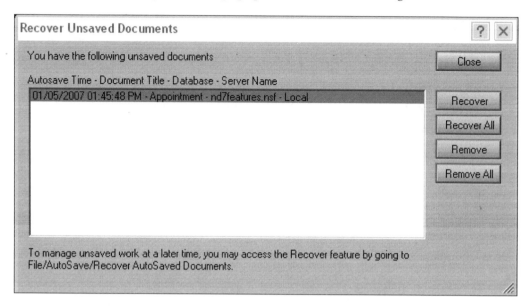

Enough information is provided in the dialog box for you to make an informed decision about whether or not to recover the document(s).

To keep the AutoSave database itself clean and fast, and to prevent the user from receiving repeat warnings about the same old documents, AutoSave documents are held in a special Notes database (.nsf file) until they are no longer needed (because the documents have been successfully saved or recovered). The database is named with a convention that allows multiple users on the same machine to have different AutoSave databases. The filename of the database is as_ followed by the first initial and then the entire last name of the user. So for user Fred Merkle, the AutoSave database would be called as_fmerkle.nsf.

Things to Consider when Enabling AutoSave in a Form

For the developer, enabling AutoSave is very easy, but there are some potential issues that you need to think about first. For example, if you enable this feature on a complex form that has a lot of event-driven code, you may not get satisfactory results. For simple forms (or forms that are complex only because they have many fields), AutoSave should work very well.

To illustrate this point about complex forms not necessarily working properly with AutoSave, imagine this scenario. You have an application applying for security clearance. A user creates a document and saves it, and the document is then reviewed by a manager. That manager can change the status from Submitted to Reviewed, Accepted, Rejected, and so on. When the status changes, an email is sent to all interested parties informing them of this change. The program tracks whether the status changes during a user session by way of a PostOpen event. It saves in memory the value of the status as the document was opened. Then, as the document is saved, the QuerySave event compares the current value to what is being held in memory (and this is the key). If the value is different, an email message is generated that says, for example, "Dear Fred Merkle, your request for security clearance Alpha has been reviewed and the status has been changed to REJECTED for the following reason: [explanation follows]".

If a manager experienced a crash while in the middle of reviewing a security request in this application, and then rebooted Notes and used AutoSave to recover their document, edits would be preserved (which of course is how AutoSave is supposed to work). However, AutoSave cannot preserve the in-memory value of the status field. In our example, this would create a problem, because the notification email would not be sent out. But in many applications, the forms do not use sophisticated in-memory tracking, and so AutoSave will work smoothly. In fact, even in our example, AutoSave will save your work; it just won't preserve the in-memory information. So although the work flow process would be compromised, at least your data would still be preserved.

The key here is that the developer needs to think about each form and whether or not the potential for data loss outweighs any potential compromises in how the application functions. In many cases, the answer is an easy yes, and so enabling this feature makes sense.

Referencing Profile Documents in Views

In Notes/Domino 6, you can reference a profile document from a view in order to determine the appropriate color choices. The mail template does this, and this allows a user to specify that emails from (for instance) Fred Merkle should appear in blue, while messages from Alice Merkle should appear in orange. This is a powerful feature for enhancing the user interface of any application.

Notes/Domino 7 takes this a step further and allows you to actually populate a view column with icons based on choices made in a profile document. We'll go through a simple example, and then we'll look at how to employ this feature.

Imagine that you've got a Sales Tracking application. There are many thousands of companies and customers and products. Each month, your management team chooses a small set of customers and products that should receive special attention. Wouldn't it be nice if there were a column that had a special icon that would display whether the record referenced that customer or product? With this new feature, you can do exactly that.

Your first steps will be to create a profile document form, and then create the appropriate labels and fields within that form. In our simple example, we might have a Company field and a Product field. These two fields might be keyword lists that reference the list of companies and products respectively.

Next, you need to create a special computed text field in this profile form that resolves to the formula you'd like to see in your view column. For example, you might want the view column formula to read as follows:

```
@if(CompanyName = <company name chosen in profile document> |
ProductName = <product chosen in profile document>; 59; 0)
```

This would display a dollar-bill icon if the company name in a record was the same as the value chosen in your profile document, or if the product chosen matched the product value in your profile document.

To make this formula, your profile-document formula might read as follows (and note the use of quotation marks):

```
"c := Company;
p := Product;

vCompanyName := \"" + CompanyName + "\";
vProductName := \"" + ProductName + "\";
@if(c = vCompanyName | p = vProductName; 59; 0)"
```

In the preceding formula, Company and Product refer to the values in the documents in the view, CompanyName and ProductName (and therefore vCompanyName and vProductName) refer to the values in the profile document.

The final step is to create a column in your view that is marked with the following Column Properties settings:

- **User definable** selected

- **Profile Document** named, for example, (**Profile-Interest**)

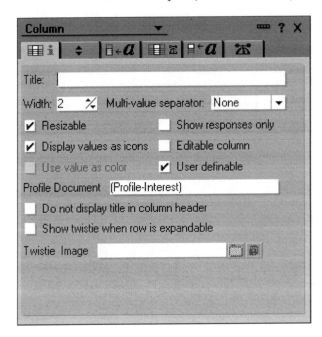

- Programmatic Name set to reference the computed text field from your profile document form, for example, **$Interest**

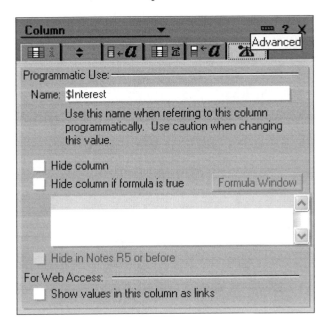

- and in the formula box for this column, enter a formula such as @Random:

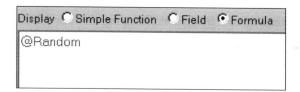

This will be overwritten with your profile-document's computed text formula, but it serves as a placeholder. If you substitute a simpler formula (such as 0), you will break the function, and all your documents in the view will display as replication/ save conflicts.

We'd like to mention two final notes about using profile documents in views (whether they are just for color or for displaying icons). First, these profile documents cannot be per user, they must be per database. Second, every time the profile document is updated, every view that references that profile document must be rebuilt (not just refreshed). So this is a very handy feature for an administrator or database owner to be able to use, but it might be dangerous if all 5,000 users of your application have access to a button that lets them update the profile document in question.

Web Services

In an ongoing effort to make Domino more compliant with open standards, Notes/ Domino 7 offers the ability to make your Domino server a hosted Web Service. This means that clients can make Web Service requests from your Domino server, just as they would from any Web Service.

In the Domino Designer 7 client, there is a new design element under **Shared Code** called **Web Services**. A Web Service design element is very similar in structure and function to an agent, and in fact, most of the user interface is the same. In particular, the **Security** tab is the same, providing restrictions on agent/Web Service activity, who can see the agent/Web Service, and whether or not this should run as a web user, as the signer of the design element, or under the authority of another user.

A significant feature of Web Services is that they return data to the requesting client as XML data.

DB2 Design Integration

In Notes/Domino 7, you have the ability to use a DB2 back-end to provide robust query capabilities across multiple Notes databases. There is some work required to set this up:

- DB2 must be installed. This does not come with Domino; it is a separate install.
- There is some Domino configuration required, mostly to set up as an authorized DB2 user account.

The Notes database(s) that you want to integrate with DB2 must be created as DB2-enabled. If you have an existing database that you want to convert, you can make a copy or replica copy and mark it as a DB2 database. (It is not possible to convert existing databases simply through your new server configuration, or through a server-console command.) In your Notes database, you can then create a DB2 Access View (DAV), which sets up the appropriate tables in the DB2 storage. Note that you may have to clean your data to avoid data-type conflicts. Also note that these will add to the size of your storage needs, but will not be reflected in the size of the database as recorded in any of the Domino housekeeping reports. However, this size is usually fairly nominal.

In your Notes database, you can now create views that use SQL statements to leverage these DAVs and which can display results from across multiple documents, even across multiple databases, for use within a single Notes view. A simple example would be a view that displays customer information as well as the internal sales rep's name from SalesActivity documents in the SalesTracking database, and also displays the sales rep's information, which comes from your SalesRepInfo database. A table similar to the one below will display in your view, with the first six columns coming from SalesTracking and the right-most column (Rep Phone) coming from SalesRepInfo.

Company	Customer	City	State	Zip	Rep	Rep Phone
ACME, Inc.	Alice Smith	Boston	MA	02100	Fred Merkle	617.555.5555
ACME, Inc.	Betty Rogers	Boston	MA	02100	Jane Merkle	617.444.4444

Tips when Using DB2

There is no direct performance gain from DB2-enabling your Notes database(s). Although the file structure of a DB2 database is far more efficient than Domino for storing large quantities of well-defined data, these gains cannot be realized by the combined setup of a DB2-enabled Domino database. On the other hand, if you have a business need for various views or reports that combine data from multiple sources (as with our simple example above), then you can consider DB2-enabling your databases as a very high-performance alternative to writing your own code to mimic this feature.

If you make a database copy (or replica copy) on a server or workstation that does not have DB2 installed, you will have to make this a regular NSF copy, and it will not have the capability to do the special SQL query views. However, your NSF data will be entirely preserved.

Template Management

When you upgrade your servers, you are likely to upgrade some or all of the standard templates: Domino Directory, Mail, Resource & Reservations, Discussion, and so on. There are three major steps you need to perform to ensure compatibility throughout your upgrade process:

1. Review code
2. Customize new templates
3. Recompile script libraries

These steps are logical and sensible, but easily overlooked in the hustle and bustle of upgrading servers, clients, and your own customized application code.

Reviewing Code

The first step is to know what code has changed between your old templates and the new (release 7) templates, and simply to test your client mix (as most customers will not upgrade every single client simultaneously) against these new features/ templates. You can determine the code differences by running a utility that will break down all design changes. (See Appendix A for more information about tools.) After you determine what code has changed, you must perform some analysis to decide what is worth testing—it's better to identify whatever errors or problems you may encounter before you upgrade.

Customizing New Templates

If you have customized your mail template, or any other standard template, you'll need to take one further step. You should have documented all of your own customizations, and now you'll need to analyze your customizations against the code changes in the new templates, and then apply your customizations appropriately to the new templates. In most cases, this presents no problems. However, sometimes design elements are added or removed, field names that you had reserved for your own use are now used by the template, or subs/functions which had been used in the old template are completely missing in the new template. So this too needs careful analysis.

Recompiling Script Libraries

Finally, for any application that has your own code, whether partly or wholly customized, you'll want to recompile all the LotusScript under Notes/Domino 7. To do this, open the **Script Libraries** view in Domino Designer, and select

Tools | Recompile All Scripts. Depending upon the size of the application, this may take some time, as it has to parse through all your code twice, once to build up a dependency tree and again to find any code problems.

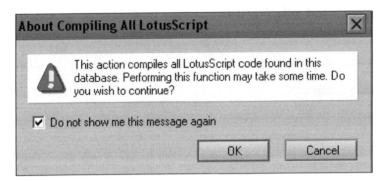

When the compiling is complete, you will be presented with a dialog box that lists the design elements with problems. You can go directly into that design element from the dialog box to fix the problems. In the following example, we have changed a script library sub that is referenced from two forms, Recompile Script1 and Recompile Script2:

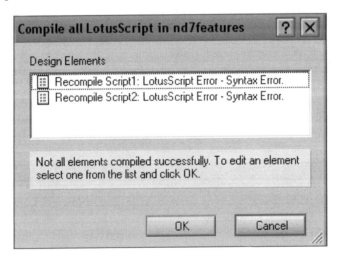

Note that if you click on one of these design elements in the dialog box and click **OK**, it will open that design element for you, but it won't put you directly into the event, button, sub, and so on that needs fixing. You'll still have to find that yourself. One way is to make a meaningless edit (such as inserting a space and then removing it) and then try to save. The form will now catch the error, so it will more helpfully point out where the error is coming from.

Note that after you finish with that form, and save and close it, you will not go back to the preceding dialog box. Instead, you'll be back in the Script Libraries view. To return to the dialog box, you will have to select **Tools | Recompile All Scripts** again.

A Final Note about Templates

If you are not experienced with templates, be careful the first few times you work with them. Templates will push changes, by default, every night into all databases referencing the templates on that server. That means that if you make changes directly to the design elements in the application, you risk having your changes overwritten by the template. Worse, if you check off the setting to prohibit design template updates, then you risk having your design out of synch with template changes.

Under Design properties in the third tab, you can select the option **Prohibit design refresh or replace to Modify**. But this risks making your design out of synch with the template. Typically, you would do this for a troubleshooting view that does not need to reside in the template.

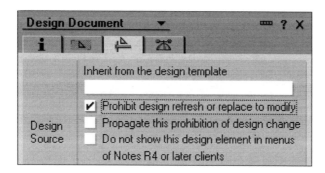

On the **Design** tab of Database properties, you can assign a template for this database. Doing so will refresh/replace all design elements in your database, as needed, from the template on that server every night.

Summary

In this chapter, we've discussed several new and enhanced Notes/Domino 7 features that raise particularly interesting application upgrade issues. These features include AutoSave, the ability to reference profile documents in views, Web Services, and DB2 integration. We also took a look at managing your Notes/Domino templates to accommodate the updates and enhancements made to them in Notes/Domino 7. This information will help ensure that your critical applications continue to run smoothly after you upgrade your Notes/Domino installation, while taking advantage of the new features and functionality release 7 has to offer.

6

Upgrading Formulas

Domino Designer 7 offers new features that enhance the @Formula language. Note, however, that using some of these features may present risks in preserving the functionality provided by existing applications. This chapter focuses on identifying and mitigating those risks.

Before you Begin: Devise a Backup Strategy

A good backup and recovery strategy should be fundamental to any upgrade campaign. Consider backing up the executable directory, the data directory, and any directory-linked folders. In short, consider backing up all your Domino-related files and data prior to your upgrade. This will allow you to restore your specific version of the Domino software, and preserve a copy of your NSF files in the ODS version you are upgrading from. This would be particularly important when upgrading from an R5.x version of the Domino software. This backup will serve as a baseline for compatibility testing your existing applications should something unanticipated occur during your upgrade.

New @Commands and @Formulas

The Domino Designer 7 provides both new @Commands and @Formulas. Many of these are oriented towards the new DB2 for Domino feature. Others simplify the design of existing applications or help leverage new features offered by Domino Designer 7. The following sections examine new @Formulas and consider their usage.

@Command([DiscoverFolders])

`@Command([DiscoverFolders])` streamlines the process of identifying the folders to which a document belongs. This function can be used by end users and helps eliminate the need for developers to program similar functionality. There are some prerequisites for its use. First, it must be called from a design element containing an **Embedded Outline** that has the **Maintain folder unread information** property enabled. This property is not available directly within an Outline design element, but is available when embedding it within another design element (see the following illustration):

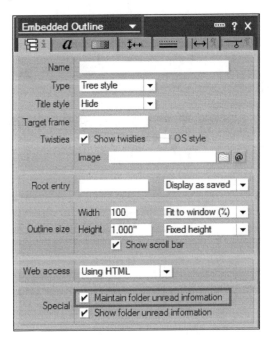

The requirements of the `DiscoverFolders` command generally dictate that it be used from within a frameset. For example, a frameset might contain a page with an embedded outline in one frame. This embedded outline must have the **Maintain folder unread information** setting set as described previously. The frameset would also contain a frame that displays a view. This view would contain a view action linked to the `DiscoverFolders` command. In the following illustration, a frameset contains a frame with a page design element with an embedded outline control, as well as a frame with a view to select documents. The `@Command([DiscoverFolders])` view action has been clicked. This displays a dialog containing (among other things) a list of folders. The folders contain the currently selected document:

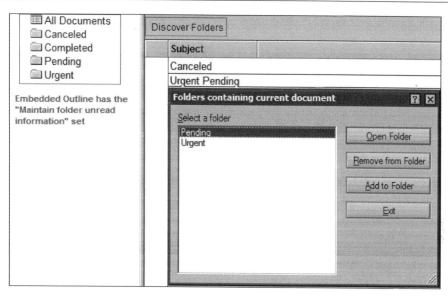

If the selected document does not occur in any folders, the action displays the following dialog:

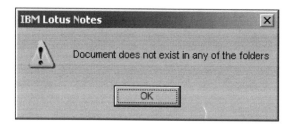

Note that, if all prerequisites for this function are not met, the Notes client returns the error: **Cannot execute the specified command**. @Command([DiscoverFolders]) does not work on the web.

@AdminECLIsLocked

@AdminECLIsLocked allows developers to determine whether the Administration ECL of the current user is locked. The Administration ECL is defined in the Domino Directory by the administrator, and is used to define which signatures can run what type of method calls. The Notes client copies this information from the server to the client during setup, and also receives ECL updates from the server if configured by the Domino administrator.

@AdminECLIsLocked is useful for determining whether updates to the Administration ECL are possible prior to attempting them. It can help prevent runtime errors when executing code that attempts to modify the Administration ECL. This function returns a Boolean value. A return value of 1 or True indicates that the Administration ECL is locked and cannot be edited. This function returns a 0 or False if the current settings do allow it to be edited. The pubnames.ntf design template leverages this new function to deliver improved manageability.

The following code sample illustrates the usage of this function:

```
@If(@AdminECLIsLocked; @Return("Administration ECL Is Locked");
@EditECL("Engineering" : "names.nsf"; "Testers"))
```

@AdminECLIsLocked does not work on the web. This is to be expected because web users are not required to have a local name and address book database.

DB2-Related @Functions

As mentioned in Chapter 3, Domino 7 introduces the ability to use IBM DB2 as a data store. To support this, four new DB2-related @Functions have been added. These include @IsDB2, @DB2Schema, @IsEmbeddedInsideWCT, and @PolicyIsFieldLocked.

@IsDB2

@IsDB2 lets you query a database to determine whether it is a DB2-backed Domino database. It provides two signatures; the first is a server and filename, and the second is a server and a replica ID. This is useful for preventing runtime errors in cases where you might not fully know which servers your code will run against. This function is particularly important if a database is replicated between a standard NSF-based Domino server and a DB2-backed Domino server.

@IsDB2 returns a 1 if the Domino database is backed by DB2 and returns a 0 if it is not. This function can be combined with @DbName to test the current database for DB2 support. @IsDB2("" : "") is equivalent to the use of @DbName.

@DB2Schema

@DB2Schema is intended for use with DB2 Access Views. It allows you to formulate SQL queries based on a DAV, without the need to know the DB2 Schema name in advance. This can be particularly useful when testing against multiple schemas; you can use @DB2Schema to formulate the SQL query at runtime. This function takes two arguments: the server name and either the filepath or the replica ID of the database.

The following formula demonstrates the use of this function to generate a runtime SQL statement for the current database:

```
RuntimeSchemaName := @DB2Schema( @DbName );
"SELECT FirstName, LastName FROM " + RuntimeSchemaName + ".dav1"
```

This @Formula could also generate either an empty string if the database in question is not a DB2-backed Domino database or an error if the server or database could not be found. Given this, it is always a good idea to trap for either an empty string or an error within your @Formula.

@IsEmbeddedInsideWCT

`@IsEmbeddedInsideWCT` determines whether the current Notes session is embedded within the Workplace client. This provides a tool to prevent an unsupported @ Formula from executing with a Notes session that is at least partially hosted by the Workplace client. The function returns a `1` if content is hosted by the Workplace client, and `0` if not.

@PolicyIsFieldLocked

`@PolicyIsFieldLocked` is used to determine whether a field is secured from updates by an administration policy. Its only argument is the name of field that is to be tested.

This function is intended for use in hide-when and input-enabled formulas. It does not function with view selection, view column, or view action formulas.

Obsolete @Formulas

Domino Designer 6 introduced the `@IfError` formula. This @Formula has been flagged as obsolete in Domino Designer 7. This @Formula still functions in Domino Designer 7, but be aware that using it may cause problems with your application over the long term. `@IsError` has been around for years and provides a fine alternative for trapping errors using the @Formula language.

Third-Party Tools

Third-party vendors offer products that help automate the process of reviewing your applications for compatibility with Domino 7 and Designer 7. These tools are geared towards businesses that need to migrate a large number of databases.

Currently, the most prominent third-party tool for helping ensure Notes/Domino 7 compatibility is Teamstudio Analyzer, (See `http://www.teamstudio.com/solutions/analyzer-spotlight.html`.) This provides a pluggable architecture that allows customers to buy only the filters they need. One such filter is Best Practices for Domino 7. They also sell filters to automate the scanning of code known to cause problems during an upgrade.

Summary

In this chapter, we examined some of the issues you need to consider when upgrading your @Formula language to Notes/Domino 7. We began by mentioning backup strategy, the most critical step you should take before undertaking any upgrade program. We then took a tour through the new Notes/Domino @Formulas and the potential upgrade issues they raise. And we mentioned `@IfError`, an existing @Formula that has been flagged as obsolete in Notes/Domino 7. Finally, we concluded with a brief mention of Teamstudio Analyzer, one of the third-party tools that can help you avoid any backward-compatibility issues when upgrading to Notes/Domino 7.

7
Upgrading Agents and LotusScript

There are a number of new LotusScript enhancements included in Domino 7. In many cases, these provide scripting access to new features. Your upgrade may provide an opportunity to leverage these. (See Chapter 4 for a complete list of new Domino Designer 7 features.)

Before You Begin

Let's begin with a few safety steps designed to increase data protection and integrity during your upgrade to Domino 7.

Design a Test Plan

A test plan is critical to any Domino upgrade. A test plan should include creating an inventory of all applications in the Domino environment. This inventory should be reviewed and prioritized to identify procedures appropriate to each application. This also provides an opportunity to identify unused applications as well as simple applications that may require no testing. Custom-built applications will require more testing than those based on standard Domino templates.

Upgrading LotusScript agents to Domino 7 should involve a thorough testing of key functions throughout all important applications. This should result in a list of actions for testers to perform in both the Release 6 and Release 7 versions of the product. Having this list ensures that you can identify measurable differences in behaviour that might occur between the two versions.

Create Backups

Backups are essential to any upgrade strategy. Always preserve an instance of your applications in the file format in which they exist prior to the upgrade. Consider additional steps such as backing up your existing applications to archive media. This ensures that you have a safe copy of the application in case you discover your application is incompatible with Domino 7. Creating redundant instances of your databases in the testing environment will also help separate testing activities from your production environment, and allow the testing databases to be discarded if necessary.

Recompile All LotusScript

LotusScript should be recompiled in the Domino 7 testing environment prior to performing any tests. This ensures that LotusScript-based design artifacts are consistent with the testing platform. This section examines how to prepare databases using the **Recompile All LotusScript** tool included in Domino Designer.

The **Recompile All LotusScript** tool first appeared in Domino Designer 6. It continues to provide a means of streamlining the validating design elements as they are updated to Domino Designer 7 format. The **Recompile All LotusScript** feature is also useful when testing the script libraries used in multiple design elements. This tool is available via the Domino Designer **Tools** menu:

Selecting this option results in the following:

1. The tool will first construct a list of all elements containing LotusScript.
2. The tool will recompile the source code.
3. The tool will then resave all design elements found in the list.

As the **Recompile All LotusScript** tool completes its work, it saves any and all design artifacts containing LotusScript. This will resave any design notes that the tool recompiles using the current user ID as well as update the Last Modified property. Consider the impact this may cause when applying this tool to active databases. To use this tool safely, make a copy of the database and invoke the **Recompile All**

LotusScript action on it. This ensures that your applications continue to work in their existing environments.

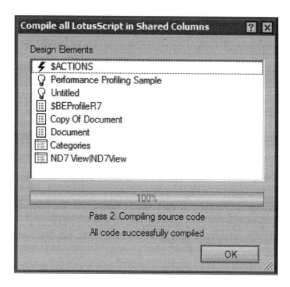

One anomaly of this feature occurs when recompiling design notes that do not contain code. If you recompile a database with an agent containing no code, it will not appear in the list of recompiled design elements, nor will it be resaved using the current user ID.

After you have prepared the databases, proceed with testing the critical components of those databases identified as important according to your test plan. A list of agents from each database provides a good starting point. A description of a successful run provides an even better baseline measurement for testing.

Other Considerations

If you are upgrading from a Domino 5.x release, review your LotusScript-based design artifacts for the + concatenation operator. Historically, BASIC-compatible languages such as LotusScript have allowed developers to concatenate strings and numeric data types with the + operator. This was done to eliminate the need to explicitly type cast variables when using concatenation operators, and encouraged less than accurate data type-casting.

Notes/Domino 6 and 7 are more restrictive in its promotion of data types when using the + operator versus the & operator. Specifically, using the + operator to concatenate strings with other numeric data types is no longer supported; a workaround is to use the & operator:

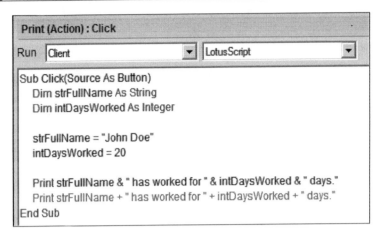

```
Print (Action) : Click
Run  Client              ▼   LotusScript          ▼

Sub Click(Source As Button)
    Dim strFullName As String
    Dim intDaysWorked As Integer

    strFullName = "John Doe"
    intDaysWorked = 20

    Print strFullName & " has worked for " & intDaysWorked & " days."
    Print strFullName + " has worked for " + intDaysWorked + " days."
End Sub
```

Third-Party Tools

Third-party tools and vendors are available to assist with planning your upgrade. These are available at a cost, but can be particularly useful for reviewing large numbers of databases to identify known issues. Teamstudio sells the Teamstudio Migration Filters that work in conjunction with the Audit feature of their Teamstudio Analyzer product. Teamstudio Filters define a set of rules to compare and report against specified Domino databases. The Teamstudio Migration Filters are a set of predefined filters that are designed specifically to streamline the Domino application upgrade process. The product also allows its users to augment the default rules by defining their own filters, making it useful not only for generating upgrade compatibility reports for large numbers of databases, but also for setting corporate standards for Domino-based applications.

Teamstudio ND7 Migration Filters define issues known to affect applications during the upgrade process. With it administrators can generate reports against databases, highlighting conditions relevant to the upgrade process. Teamstudio Analyzer creates an analysis of the application which the filters are applied against to highlight design elements requiring attention. The filters act as customizable semaphores. If your organization is not interested in a specific filter, it can be disabled without the need to delete it.

Teamstudio sells predefined filter sets designed to streamline specific administrative tasks. When generating a report, you select a filter database and a filter set, and additionally select a database to receive the results of the report.

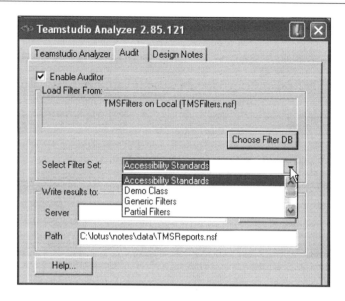

The following screenshot illustrates the ND7 Migration Filters database. This set of Filters is a Teamstudio product focused towards customers who wish to automate the identifying of design elements that require additional attention during the upgrade process:

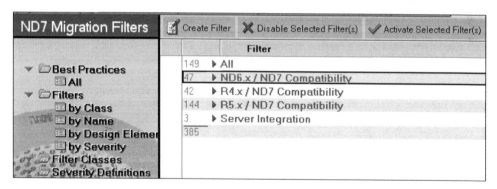

Each Migration Filter attempts to flag specific issues that can occur as a result of the upgrade. The following screenshot displays a filter document that identifies a code combination known to cause issues during an upgrade:

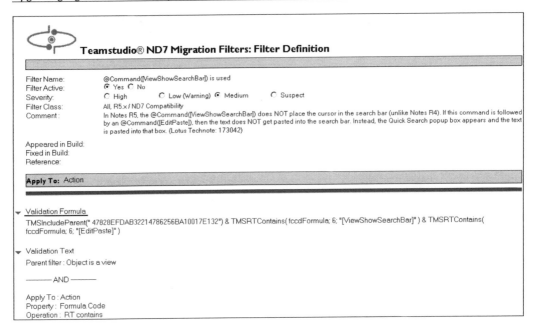

After you select a filter set, you can run them against databases to generate a report. This report is output into a Teamstudio results database. The following screenshot identifies a sample report output for review by an administrator:

Class	Element	Found In	Filter
▼ TSD Sales Template			
▼ 10/31/2006 11:24:13 AM			
▼ Coding			
	US Quotation	TSD Sales Templat	Each Form should have a Window Title
	Form	US Quotation	Comments Should Not Be Used in the @Formula Language
	TextDate	US Quotation	Field has no input translation formula
	CompanyName	US Quotation	Field has no input translation formula
	ContactName	US Quotation	Field has no input translation formula

Teamstudio offers other filter sets that allow customers to further leverage their investment in the Analyzer beyond the Migration Filters. The following shows their **Best Practices Filters**:

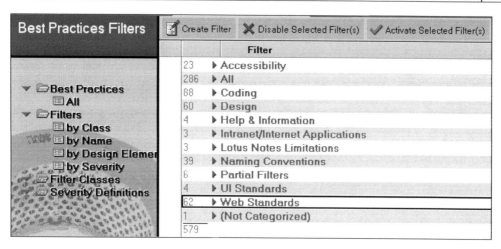

Administrators and developers can create their own filters, allowing users to extend the product by defining their own filters to reflect corporate coding guidelines and best practices. The following shows the form that provides customers with this functionality:

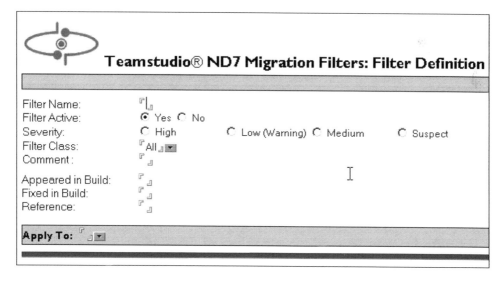

For further information on Teamstudio Analyzer and Teamstudio Migration Filters, visit their site at `http://www.teamstudio.com/migration`.

New Features

The remainder of this chapter focuses on the new LotusScript and agent features available in Notes/Domino 7. Some of these features may allow you to simplify existing designs. Others are designed to simplify tasks related to maintaining and monitoring your code.

Profiling

Domino 7 provides developers with product-based tools to profile agent performance. Profiling allows developers and administrators to gather data about the time required to make calls to Domino objects as well as identify possible bottlenecks in code that is performing poorly. Domino 7 profiling eliminates the need for a developer to code these features by hand or clutter up agent design with code designed only to measure performance. Web services can also be profiled (see Chapter 8).

Profiling data should only be collected while troubleshooting code or identifying bottlenecks. Profiling creates its own overhead and can compromise security in a production environment. To profile an agent, open it in Domino Designer 7 and select **Agent** Properties. Click the **Security** tab, and enable the **Profile this agent** setting.

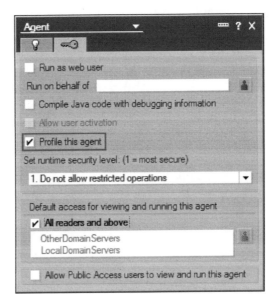

Only LotusScript and Java agents can be profiled, imported Java agents can not be profiled.

After an agent has been enabled for profiling, its performance data is collected the next time it is run. Profile documents are saved with a form field value of $BEProfileR7. This form is hidden from view within Domino Designer 7.

To view profiling results using Domino Designer 7, select the **Agent** in the Agents View, and click **View Profile Results**.

This opens the profile document for the selected agent, if it exists. A sample profile document appears as follows:

Performance Measurements Profile

10/17/2006 11:12:45 PM EDT
Elapsed time: 30 msec
Methods profiled: 2
Total measured time: 10 msec

Class	Method	Operation	Calls	Time
Session	CurrentDatabase	Get	1	10
Database	Title	Get	1	0

The following list identifies the information collected in the profile document:

- **Class** is the name of the Domino object class using standardized names. Actual variable names are not provided.

- **Method** is the Domino object's method or property using class-member names, not variable names.

- **Operation** indicates whether or not a Get or Set method was used.

- **Calls** is the number of invocations for the specified method or property.

- **Time** is the amount of time required to complete the operation. The symbol < indicates that the operation was completed with insufficient time to allow measuring it with accuracy.

Developers using the Designer 7 client menu to view profiling data can request to view performance data for agents that have not yet collected the requested data. The **View Profile Results** dialog displays the following dialog if profiling data has not been collected since the agent was last saved:

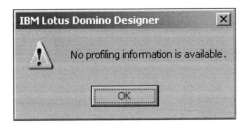

Profiling data is purged each time an agent is saved. An agent must be run again after resaving to collect profiling data. Profiling data is collected for agents regardless of whether they run on a server or via the Lotus Notes 7 client. In addition to using the Designer 7 client menu to view profiling data, new method calls also allow programmatic display. This is covered in the following section.

New LotusScript Methods

Domino Designer 7 offers a number of new LotusScript methods. This section examines these methods and discusses their possible uses.

NotesDatabase.GetModifiedDocuments([ndtSince], [intClass])

GetModifiedDocuments is a new LotusScript method used to obtain any data or design elements modified after a given date/time. Its method signature is:

```
NotesDocumentCollection =
            NotesDatabase.GetModifiedDocuments([ndtSince], [intClass])
```

This function returns a NotesDocumentCollection object of matching elements. Both arguments (ndtSince and intClass) are optional. The first argument, if specified, is a NotesDateTime object indicating a cutoff date. If specified, any documents modified prior to this time are not included in the return object. If the first argument is not specified, this call will return all documents matching the data passed in the second argument. The second argument is an integer used to specify the types of elements to be returned in the NotesDocumentCollection object. A set of constants are used to specify what types of elements to return. These are:

- DBMOD_DOC_ACL (64)
- DBMOD_DOC_AGENT (512)
- DBMOD_DOC_ALL (32767)
- DBMOD_DOC_DATA (1)
- DBMOD_DOC_FORM (4)
- DBMOD_DOC_HELP (256)
- DBMOD_DOC_ICON (16)
- DBMOD_DOC_REPLFORMULA (2048)
- DBMOD_DOC_SHAREDFIELD (1024)
- DBMOD_DOC_VIEW (8)

The default value for this function is DBMOD_DOC_DATA or 1, which returns data documents. The preceding constants can be combined using a logical OR to return more than one element type. If neither argument is specified, the function call returns a NotesDocumentCollection object with all data documents in the database.

The NotesDatabase.GetModifiedDocuments function is useful for obtaining a set of design elements or documents that have been updated since a given time. Possible examples include calls to locate documents since an agent was last run, or design elements modified after a given date time. It can provide other uses in queries made by end users. When using this function, it is important to understand whether scheduled agents update the data periodically, and whether it does it on an as-needed basis or indiscriminately. Scheduled agents that update documents indiscriminately undermine the usefulness of this method. If you intend to use this function, it is a good practice to update only data that needs updating to ensure that the function can filter data effectively.

NotesDocumentCollection.UntilTime

The NotesDocumentCollection.UntilTime property returns a NotesDateTime object indicating the cutoff time for the NotesDocumentCollections object obtained using the NotesDatabase.GetModifiedDocuments function. This property applies only to those document collections obtained using the

`NotesDatabase.GetModifiedDocuments` function. Accessing this property for document collections instantiated by other means causes this property to return an empty string.

NotesUIWorkspace.IsEmbeddedInsideWCT

The `IsEmbeddedInsideWCT` property of the `NotesUIWorkspace` class is used to determine whether or not an application is running in the IBM Workplace client. If `true`, this property indicates that the code is running from within the Workplace client and not the Lotus Notes client. This function helps applications adjust to deployment in the Workplace client by allowing the developer to take context-sensitive actions depending on the client hosting the code.

NotesAgent.GetPerformanceDocument

The `GetPerformanceDocument` method of the `NotesAgent` class is used to programmatically access profiling results associated with the `NotesAgent` on which the method is invoked, if they are available. If profiling results are not available for the `NotesAgent` object, the method returns `Nothing`. The method's return value should be tested for this to prevent runtime errors. The following code snippet illustrates this:

```
Set docProfileResults = agent.GetPerformanceDocument
If docProfileResults Is Nothing Then
   ' *** no profiling results are available
Else
   ' *** profiling results are available
End If
```

If an agent is resaved, its profiling data is cleared until the next time the agent is run.

LotusScript Debugger

Domino Designer 7 contains debugger enhancements intended to simplify the debugging process. These include a SmartIcon that can be used to enable or disable the debugger. This icon can be seen in the toolbar and appears in the following screenshot:

It is a toggle operation; clicking it the first time enables the debugger, and clicking it a second time disables the debugger. If you are unsure about the debugger's state, check the status bar. In Designer 7, a message appears each time the debugger icon or menu item is clicked identifying its state.

LotusScript debugging started

Agent Design View

Domino Designer 7 provides an enhanced agent design view. Like other design views, it allows the developer to edit basic attributes of the design note without the need to fully open them in its editor. Column attributes denoting whether the agent is private, how it is triggered, and whether or not the designer task can update it have been converted from textual to graphical descriptions. The column-header descriptions for "Notes" and "Web" runtime targets have also been converted from text to icons. This allows the agent design view to add a **Comments** column to display developers' comments directly in the view. This eliminates the need to open agents individually using the design editor and view that information via the infobox. For databases where agents are commented, this provides a quick summarized view of all the agents' comments available for printing.

Summary

This chapter outlined steps for planning an upgrade to LotusScript and Domino based agents. These included formulating a test plan and identifying measurements to ensure your agents perform consistently in Domino 7. It also made suggestions for creating backups and archival copies should they be needed. It concluded with an examination of the new features available to LotusScript developers in Domino Designer 7.

Web Services and Domino 7

8

Web services are loosely coupled autonomous web applications that integrate with other web applications, without the need to build custom-connection code. Domino 7 extends its embrace of open standards by adding formalized support for web services. Web services can extend the reach of your existing Domino applications, as well as provide new applications with industry-standard integration points.

Before discussing Domino-based web services, let's first identify a few characteristics that apply generally to web services. Web services consist of service providers and service consumers. They are made possible by a set of technologies used to build programmatic interfaces for systems to communicate data on a network:

XML (Extensible Markup Language) is used to encode structured data to form the request and response information exchanged between the web-service client and the web-service provider. As it is text based, it is portable across platforms and easily read by a variety of tools. This eliminates the need for binary compatibility.

SOAP (Simple Object Access Protocol) is a messaging protocol used to package XML.

WSDL (Web Services Description Language) is an XML-based standard used to describe the various inputs and outputs that a web-service provider supports. A web-service provider publishes a WSDL document that describes the web-service interface by specifying supported service operations, as well as the response format for each operation, effectively encapsulating the runtime implementation.

UDDI (Universal Description, Discovery, and Integration) is an XML-based protocol used to allow organizations to catalog and publish their services and asynchronously discover web services published by other organizations. UDDI is *not* a required component for implementing web services. It is an optional component that facilitates the discovery and adoption of public third-party services.

The technologies that comprise web services provide for machine-to-machine communication in a platform-independent manner. Because the interface is described using text-based XML, any system that can read this format can form communication points with other systems. A web-service's implementation can still take advantage of object-oriented languages. A web-service consumer is not interested in the implementation details and is satisfied by the interface described in an XML-based WSDL document.

There are many tools from an array of vendors that specialize in hosting and consuming web services. Each can publish or consume web services in a plug-and-play fashion. Some tools are focused specifically on this task, and can incidentally connect with and communicate with Domino. Given this, it is natural to ask, "Why should I host web services in Domino?" To help answer that question, consider the following:

- Domino-based web services provide native access to Domino data. This simplifies the implementation of business logic for web services hosted by Domino.

- Domino-based web services are developed directly within a Domino database. This means that they can leverage other product features such as Domino replication and security.

- Domino-based web services can take advantage of other features native to Domino such as template management.

- Domino-based web services allow Domino administrators to leverage their expertise in maintaining security and application integrity.

- Domino-based web services can be implemented using either LotusScript or Java. This allows developers to pick the language that best suits their requirements and skills.

Creating a Simple Web Service Using Domino Designer 7

Let's examine the process for creating a simple functional web-service provider using Domino Designer 7. For this example, we will create the following Company Profile document type:

Company Profile	
Company:	Company ⊤
Ticker Symbol:	Symbol ⊤
Number of Employees:	EmployeeCount ⊤
Dividend	Dividend #
Public Float	PublicFloat #
Short Interest:	ShortInterest #

We will also load several Company Profiles into the database to demonstrate the use of the web service:

Company	Symbol	Employee Count	Dividend	Public Float	Short Interest
Landscape MD	LMD	10	1.00	100	0
Zlobek Enterprises	ZLO	1000	0.50	10000000	350000
Milo Materials	MILO	100	0.05	100000	6500

To begin creating the web-service provider interface for this application, open Domino Designer 7 to the Web Service Design view by clicking **Shared Code | Web Services**:

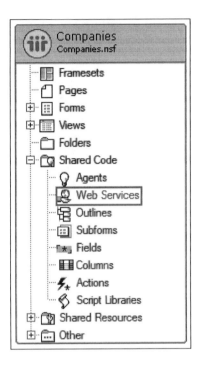

From the Web Service design view, click **New Web Service**:

This opens the Web Service design editor. In either case, the web service must define a class that receives and processes the requests made by a web service client. This class name is defined in the web service's **PortType class** field in the **Basics** tab of the web service's properties. The web service can define other classes that are used internally, but the **PortType class** defines the web-service's interface. The public methods of this class become the service operations supported by the web service. For this example, we will define a class called CompanyInfo to handle the requests made to it. The setting required for this is shown in the screenshot that follows:

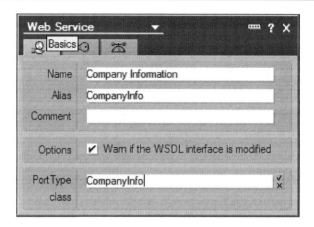

Also note that the setting **Warn if the WSDL interface is modified** is enabled. This setting is useful in cases where a web service has been deployed and web-service clients are already connecting to it. It warns the developer if code changes made to the Port Type class alter the interface published to web-service clients.

When the setting **Warn if the WSDL interface is modified** is enabled, Domino Designer 7 presents the following dialog when updating class-member functions or their signatures, indicating that the web service will not be saved:

To prevent inconvenience to the developer, this setting should be enabled only after the web service has been published.

Implementing a Simple Web Service

To begin this example, we will construct a web service with a single operation. It will receive a ticker symbol and perform a view lookup to locate a matching company name. The following code implements this functionality:

```
Dim session As NotesSession

Class CompanyInfo

    Sub NEW
```

```
            Set session = New NotesSession
        End Sub

        Function GetCompanyName(strSymbol As String) As String
            Dim dbCurrent As NotesDatabase
            Dim viewCompanyProfileLookup As NotesView
            Dim docCompanyProfile As NotesDocument

            Set dbCurrent = session.CurrentDatabase
            Set viewCompanyProfileLookup =
                            dbCurrent.GetView("CompanyProfileLookup")
            Set docCompanyProfile =
                viewCompanyProfileLookup.GetDocumentByKey(strSymbol)

            If (docCompanyProfile Is Nothing) Then
                ' *** no match found
                GetCompanyName = "No match found for " & strSymbol
            Else
                GetCompanyName =
                            docCompanyProfile.GetItemValue("Company")(0)
            End If
        End Function
    End Class
```

After saving the web service, Domino Designer 7 populates the **Advance** tab of the web service's properties with information about the web service. These can be customized, if necessary. For this example, we will use the default settings used by Domino Designer 7, with **Programming model** set to **RPC** and **SOAP message format** set to **RPC/encoded**. These can be modified as required.

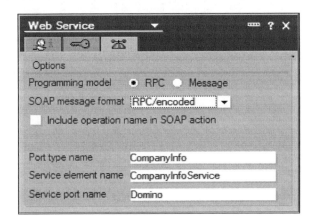

RPC/encoded is the most easily understood format. For a complete discussion on the various strengths and weaknesses of the **Programming model** and **SOAP message format** settings, refer to the document, "Which style of WSDL should I use?" at `http://www-128.ibm.com/developerworks/webservices/library/ws-whichwsdl/#N10048`.

Exploring the Web Service Using a Browser

A Domino-based web-service interface can be viewed using URLs that have the following format:

`http://servername/database.nsf/webservicename?openwebservice`

For this example, you can browse the web-service interface and see the method created earlier in the example. This Domino-generated page enumerates the public methods exposed by the web service and provides a link to browse the WSDL document that defines the web service's interface.

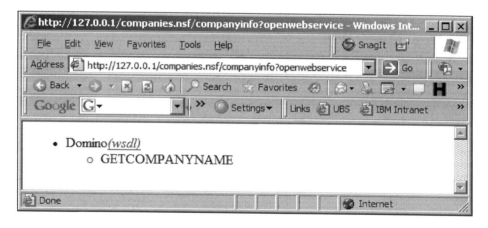

The URLs of WSDL documents for Domino-based web services have the following format:

`http://hostname/database.nsf/webservice?wsdl`

This URL is used by web-service clients to identify the web service. Development tools typically use this URL to auto-generate a basic web-service client that can then be further customized. The following code identifies the contents of this link. It describes the interface for the basic web service we just developed. There is an entry for the `GetCompanyName` operation with its `strSymbol` argument. The information provided in the WSDL allows a web-service client development tool to auto-generate a skeletal testing user interface to invoke the operations and examine their return values. No connection code is required by the developer to do this. Because the interface is described using text-based XML, testing tools can accomplish this feat across platforms.

```xml
<?xml version="1.0" encoding="UTF-8" ?>
- <wsdl:definitions targetNamespace="urn:DefaultNamespace" xmlns="http://schemas.xmlsoap.org/wsdl/"
    xmlns:apachesoap="http://xml.apache.org/xml-soap" xmlns:impl="urn:DefaultNamespace"
    xmlns:intf="urn:DefaultNamespace" xmlns:soapenc="http://schemas.xmlsoap.org/soap/encoding/"
    xmlns:wsdl="http://schemas.xmlsoap.org/wsdl/" xmlns:wsdlsoap="http://schemas.xmlsoap.org/wsdl/soap/"
    xmlns:xsd="http://www.w3.org/2001/XMLSchema">
  - <wsdl:message name="GETCOMPANYNAMERequest">
      <wsdl:part name="STRSYMBOL" type="xsd:string" />
    </wsdl:message>
  - <wsdl:message name="GETCOMPANYNAMEResponse">
      <wsdl:part name="GETCOMPANYNAMEReturn" type="xsd:string" />
    </wsdl:message>
  - <wsdl:portType name="CompanyInfo">
    - <wsdl:operation name="GETCOMPANYNAME" parameterOrder="STRSYMBOL">
        <wsdl:input message="impl:GETCOMPANYNAMERequest" name="GETCOMPANYNAMERequest" />
        <wsdl:output message="impl:GETCOMPANYNAMEResponse" name="GETCOMPANYNAMEResponse" />
      </wsdl:operation>
    </wsdl:portType>
  - <wsdl:binding name="DominoSoapBinding" type="impl:CompanyInfo">
      <wsdlsoap:binding style="rpc" transport="http://schemas.xmlsoap.org/soap/http" />
    - <wsdl:operation name="GETCOMPANYNAME">
        <wsdlsoap:operation soapAction="" />
      - <wsdl:input name="GETCOMPANYNAMERequest">
          <wsdlsoap:body encodingStyle="http://schemas.xmlsoap.org/soap/encoding/"
            namespace="urn:DefaultNamespace" use="encoded" />
        </wsdl:input>
      - <wsdl:output name="GETCOMPANYNAMEResponse">
          <wsdlsoap:body encodingStyle="http://schemas.xmlsoap.org/soap/encoding/"
            namespace="urn:DefaultNamespace" use="encoded" />
        </wsdl:output>
      </wsdl:operation>
    </wsdl:binding>
  - <wsdl:service name="CompanyInfoService">
    - <wsdl:port binding="impl:DominoSoapBinding" name="Domino">
        <wsdlsoap:address location="http://127.0.0.1:80/companies.nsf/companyinfo?OpenWebService" />
      </wsdl:port>
    </wsdl:service>
  </wsdl:definitions>
```

Next we will test the basic web service using **Rational Application Developer's Web Services Explorer**. This tool provides a means to browse and test web services using UDDI registries, WSDL documents, and WSIL documents. There are multiple ways to launch the Web Services Explorer. In this example, we launch the Web Services Explorer using the **Run | Launch the Web Services Explorer** menu option. If this option does not appear, it is likely not to be enabled. To enable it, select **File | Import** and click on **Web Services** in the resulting dialog box. This will prompt you to add web-service support to the workspace. Once complete, the **Run | Launch the Web Services Explorer** menu option should appear as follows:

This opens the Web Services Explorer. The default-page view consists of a UDDI Web Service browser. To explore the `CompanyInfo` service using WSDL, click the **WSDL Page** icon located at the top right of the auto-generated page. This opens a page containing an input field for the **WSDL URL**. These elements appear as follows:

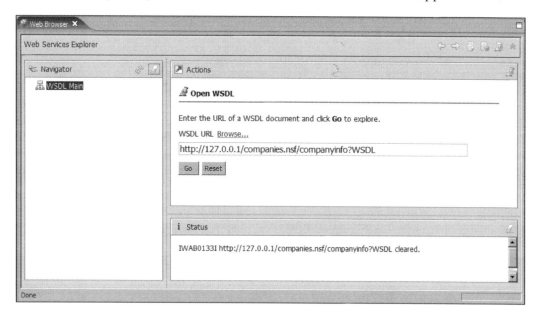

When using the Rational Application Developer's Web Services Explorer to test a Domino-based web service, the target database should allow Anonymous access. This is because the Web Services Explorer does not prompt the user for security credentials. After you have finished testing your web service, you can once again restrict Anonymous access to the database hosting the web service.

Clicking the **Go** button loads a list of operations provided by the web service. For the basic web service developed for this example, we see the **GETCOMPANYNAME** operation:

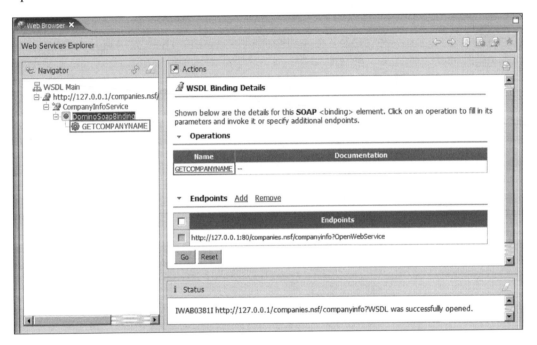

Clicking the **GETCOMPANYNAME** link generated by the Web Services Explorer opens a page containing an auto-generated input field to supply the Symbol argument needed for the method signature. In the following example, **MILO** was entered, based on test data previously entered into the database. Clicking the **Go** button invokes the web-service operation with the supplied argument. The return value **Milo Materials** is in turn displayed in the Status panel:

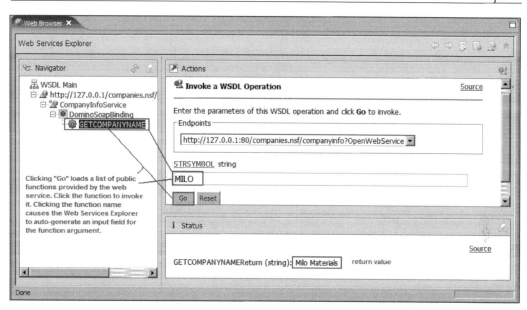

Clicking the **Source** link in the Status panel allows you to view the SOAP request generated by the Web Services Explorer, as well as the SOAP response generated by the Domino hosted web service.

The SOAP request generated by the Web Services Explorer is as follows:

```
<?xml version="1.0" encoding="UTF-8" ?>
- <SOAP-ENV:Envelope xmlns:SOAP-
  ENV="http://schemas.xmlsoap.org/soap/envelope/"
  xmlns:xsd="http://www.w3.org/2001/XMLSchema"
  xmlns:xsi="http://www.w3.org/2001/XMLSchema-instance">
  - <SOAP-ENV:Body>
    - <ns0:getCompanyName xmlns:ns0="urn:DefaultNamespace" SOAP-
      ENV:encodingStyle="http://schemas.xmlsoap.org/soap/encoding/">
      <strSymbol xsi:type="xsd:string">MILO</strSymbol>
      </ns0:getCompanyName>
  </SOAP-ENV:Body>
  </SOAP-ENV:Envelope>
```

And this is the SOAP response generated by Domino:

```
- <soapenv:Envelope
  xmlns:soapenv="http://schemas.xmlsoap.org/soap/envelope/"
  xmlns:xsd="http://www.w3.org/2001/XMLSchema"
  xmlns:xsi="http://www.w3.org/2001/XMLSchema-instance">
  - <soapenv:Body>
```

```
   -  <ns1:getCompanyNameResponse xmlns:ns1="urn:DefaultNamespace"
      soapenv:encodingStyle=
                      "http://schemas.xmlsoap.org/soap/encoding/">
      <getCompanyNameReturn xsi:type="xsd:string">Milo
      Materials</getCompanyNameReturn>
      </ns1:getCompanyNameResponse>
      </soapenv:Body>
   </soapenv:Envelope>
```

We have just examined how web services allow web applications to communicate with no connection code required. Because web services use text-based XML interface descriptions, development tools can browse the operations provided by web services in a platform neutral manner. After you publish a web service, web-service consumers can enumerate and invoke a web-service provider's operations. We will now proceed to expand the operations hosted by the web-service provider.

Adding Exception Handling to the Web Service

Currently, our CompanyInfo web-service implementation returns a string message for cases where a ticker symbol that is not in the database is entered. It is entirely possible that we might want to generate an exception under such circumstances. LotusScript does not support exception handling, but does support error handling. Unfortunately, this is not what is needed for passing an exception back to a web-service client. To address this situation, we use the new FAULT object. The following update to our implementation identifies a means to pass an exception back to the web-service client:

```
%INCLUDE "lsxsd.lss"

Dim session As NotesSession

Class CompanyInfo

  Sub NEW
    Set session = New NotesSession
  End Sub

  Function GetCompanyName(strSymbol As String,   FAULT As WS_FAULT)
                                                        As String

    Dim dbCurrent As NotesDatabase
    Dim viewCompanyProfileLookup As NotesView
    Dim docCompanyProfile As NotesDocument
```

```
      Set dbCurrent = session.CurrentDatabase
      Set viewCompanyProfileLookup =
                             dbCurrent.GetView("CompanyProfileLookup")
      Set docCompanyProfile =
                   viewCompanyProfileLookup.GetDocumentByKey(strSymbol)

      If (docCompanyProfile Is Nothing) Then
        ' *** no match found. raise an exception
        FAULT.setFault(True)
        Call FAULT.setFaultString("No match found for " & strSymbol)
      Else
        GetCompanyName = docCompanyProfile.GetItemValue("Company")(0)
      End If
    End Function
  End Class
```

A few things to consider about the previous code:

- The WS_FAULT object requires the %INCLUDE "lsxsd.lss" appearing in the first line of the code listing.

- WS_FAULT is imported via an INCLUDE statement. It therefore is not supported by the type-ahead feature.

- The WS_FAULT object is added to our GetCompanyName method signature implementation. It is not visible to web-service clients, which do not need to pass an argument for it to the method call.

Handling the "document not found" condition now means that the exception message is no longer passed back to the web-service caller as a string in the return value of the function. This provides the client a means to differentiate the "company not found" message from a valid company name, and can prevent it from processing the exception as such. The exception is now passed in the SOAP response as a faultcode element. This condition is illustrated in the following SOAP response:

```
- <soapenv:Envelope
    xmlns:soapenv="http://schemas.xmlsoap.org/soap/envelope/"
    xmlns:xsd="http://www.w3.org/2001/XMLSchema"
    xmlns:xsi="http://www.w3.org/2001/XMLSchema-instance">
  - <soapenv:Body>
    - <soapenv:Fault>
        <faultcode>soapenv:Server.generalException</faultcode>
        <faultstring>No match found for fdfd</faultstring>
        <detail />
      </soapenv:Fault>
    </soapenv:Body>
  </soapenv:Envelope>
```

Expanding the Web Service to Include Complex Data Types

We will now proceed to expand the web service by adding functions to return more data about a company. To do so, we will add a new document type called Telephone Number to store telephone numbers related to specific companies. This will be a one-to-many relationship, where each company will be joined to many telephone numbers using the symbol field. Using the telephone number, we will demonstrate how to use web services to return complex data types such as arrays.

The Telephone Number entity used for this example defines two fields:

Telephone Number	
Symbol:	Symbol T
TelephoneNumber:	TelephoneNumber T

In order to generate an array of strings to be returned by the CompanyInfo web service, we will load the following telephone-number data into the Company database:

New Telephone Number	
Symbol	**Telephone Number**
MILO	800 555 1212
MILO	804 555 1212
MILO	877 328 7448
ZLO	804 844 3711

Here is the updated web-service code to return a string array of telephone numbers, as well as a Long value indicating a company's Short Interest. A description of the changes follows the code listing:

```
%INCLUDE "lsxsd.lss"

Dim session As NotesSession

Class TelephoneNumberInfo
  Public TelephoneNumbers() As String
End Class

Class CompanyInfo
  Sub NEW
    Set session = New NotesSession
```

```
End Sub

Function GetCompanyName(strSymbol As String, FAULT As WS_FAULT)
                                                    As String
   Dim dbCurrent As NotesDatabase
   Dim viewCompanyProfileLookup As NotesView
   Dim docCompanyProfile As NotesDocument

   Set dbCurrent = session.CurrentDatabase
   Set viewCompanyProfileLookup =
                    dbCurrent.GetView("CompanyProfileLookup")
   Set docCompanyProfile =
           viewCompanyProfileLookup.GetDocumentByKey(strSymbol)

     If (docCompanyProfile Is Nothing) Then
       ' *** no match found
       FAULT.setFault(True)
       Call FAULT.setFaultString("No match found for " & strSymbol)
     Else
       GetCompanyName =
                    docCompanyProfile.GetItemValue("Company")(0)
     End If
End Function

Function GetTelephoneNumbers(strSymbol As String, FAULT As
                              WS_FAULT) As TelephoneNumberInfo
   Dim dbCurrent As NotesDatabase
   Dim viewTelephoneNumbersLookup As NotesView
   Dim dcTelephoneNumbers As NotesDocumentCollection
   Dim docTelephoneNumber As NotesDocument
   Dim intDocument As Integer
   Dim TelephoneNumbers As TelephoneNumberInfo

   Set dbCurrent = session.CurrentDatabase
   Set viewTelephoneNumbersLookup =
                    dbCurrent.GetView("TelephoneNumbersLookup")
   Set dcTelephoneNumbers =
       viewTelephoneNumbersLookup.GetAllDocumentsByKey(strSymbol)
   Set TelephoneNumbers = New TelephoneNumberInfo()

     If dcTelephoneNumbers.Count > 0 Then
       Redim TelephoneNumbers.TelephoneNumbers(1 To
                                        dcTelephoneNumbers.Count)
       For intDocument = 1 To dcTelephoneNumbers.Count
         Set docTelephoneNumber =
                    dcTelephoneNumbers.GetNthDocument(intDocument)
         TelephoneNumbers.TelephoneNumbers(intDocument) =
```

```
                    docTelephoneNumber.GetItemValue("TelephoneNumber")(0)
        Next

      Else
        Redim TelephoneNumbers.TelephoneNumbers(1 To 1)
        TelephoneNumbers.TelephoneNumbers(1) =
                          "No Telephone Numbers Available"
      End If

    Set GetTelephoneNumbers = TelephoneNumbers

  End Function

  Function GetShortInterest(strSymbol As String, FAULT As WS_FAULT)
                                                           As Long

    Dim dbCurrent As NotesDatabase
    Dim viewCompanyProfileLookup As NotesView
    Dim docCompanyProfile As NotesDocument

    Set dbCurrent = session.CurrentDatabase
    Set viewCompanyProfileLookup =
                    dbCurrent.GetView("CompanyProfileLookup")
    Set docCompanyProfile =
              viewCompanyProfileLookup.GetDocumentByKey(strSymbol)

    If (docCompanyProfile Is Nothing) Then
      ' *** no match found
      FAULT.setFault(True)
      Call FAULT.setFaultString("No match found for " & strSymbol)
    Else
      GetShortInterest =
                docCompanyProfile.GetItemValue("ShortInterest")(0)
    End If
  End Function
End Class
```

In the preceding code, it would be tempting to define the GetTelephoneNumbers function as a variant and assign a string array to it. The problem with declaring the return value of GetTelephoneNumbers as variant and assigning a string array to it is that the variant data type is too loosely typed. Variants can reference a variety of data types such as simple data types, arrays, and COM objects. Because of this, variants cannot be accurately described using WSDL. The solution to this is to declare the TelephoneNumberInfo class. It in turn defines Public member variables that become the return values to any web-service function that returns the Class type. In this case, the TelephoneNumberInfo class defines a Public string-array member variable that becomes the return value for the GetTelephoneNumbers web-service operation.

One other change to the preceding code listing is noteworthy. The web-service class handler has declared a `NotesSession` member variable. The Class's `New` method, which is called when the web service is loaded, initializes the `NotesSession` object so that it can be accessed by all member functions.

```
Sub NEW
Set session = New NotesSession
End Sub
```

This eliminates the need to create a new `NotesSession` object during each web-service function invocation.

Finally, we must note that the `TelephoneNumberInfo` class should be defined before the PortType Class that returns this object type. The LotusScript compiler generates a compile-time error if the web-service return-type `Class` is defined after the web-service implementation class, even if it is syntactically correct.

> The Class types returned by a web service should be defined prior to the web-service implementation class.

Now that, we have a class to return a string array of `TelephoneNumbers`, let's see it in action using the Rational Web Services Explorer:

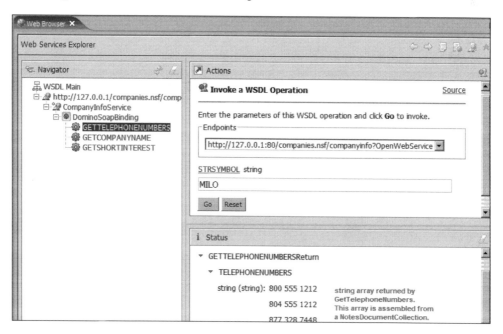

Note that in the preceding screenshot, the new GetShortInterest function also appears. This function returns numeric data cast in LotusScript using a Long data type.

We have seen how to return a string array using a web service. For the next exercise, we will return another complex type that consists of multiple data types within a single web-service response.

Other Complex Return Types

There are many cases where a web service needs to return a group of values in a single response. This response may consist of multiple values of varying data types. This is accomplished in a similar fashion to returning arrays. For the next example, we will return a complex data type called Address, consisting of multiple strings and a numeric value within a single response. For this example, we will use the following document type:

Address	
Symbol:	Symbol T
Street:	Street T
City:	City T
State:	State T
Zip:	Zip #

 Zip is defined as a numeric for demonstration purposes.

We will also use the following data for this example:

Symbol	Street	City	State	Zip
ZLO	1500 Levenston Ave	Richmond	VA	23229

We will update the web service by adding an AddressInfo class to capture this data from Domino and add a GetAddress function to the web-service class handler to return the data to web-service client requests.

Here is the updated code listing:

```
%INCLUDE "lsxsd.lss"

Dim session As NotesSession

Class TelephoneNumberInfo
  Public TelephoneNumbers() As String
End Class

Class AddressInfo
  Public Street As String
  Public City As String
  Public Zip As Long
  Public State As String
End Class

Class CompanyInfo
  Sub NEW
    Set session = New NotesSession
  End Sub

  Function GetCompanyName(strSymbol As String, FAULT As WS_FAULT)
                                                    As String
    Dim dbCurrent As NotesDatabase
    Dim viewCompanyProfileLookup As NotesView
    Dim docCompanyProfile As NotesDocument

    Set dbCurrent = session.CurrentDatabase
    Set viewCompanyProfileLookup =
                    dbCurrent.GetView("CompanyProfileLookup")
    Set docCompanyProfile =
            viewCompanyProfileLookup.GetDocumentByKey(strSymbol)

    If (docCompanyProfile Is Nothing) Then
      ' *** no match found
      FAULT.setFault(True)
      Call FAULT.setFaultString("No match found for " & strSymbol)
    Else
      GetCompanyName = docCompanyProfile.GetItemValue("Company")(0)
    End If
  End Function

  Function GetTelephoneNumbers(strSymbol As String,
                    FAULT As WS_FAULT) As TelephoneNumberInfo
    Dim dbCurrent As NotesDatabase
```

```
       Dim viewTelephoneNumbersLookup As NotesView
       Dim dcTelephoneNumbers As NotesDocumentCollection
       Dim docTelephoneNumber As NotesDocument
       Dim intDocument As Integer
       Dim TelephoneNumbers As TelephoneNumberInfo

       Set dbCurrent = session.CurrentDatabase
       Set viewTelephoneNumbersLookup =
  dbCurrent.GetView("TelephoneNumbersLookup")
       Set dcTelephoneNumbers =
            viewTelephoneNumbersLookup.GetAllDocumentsByKey(strSymbol)
       Set TelephoneNumbers = New TelephoneNumberInfo()

       If dcTelephoneNumbers.Count > 0 Then

         Redim TelephoneNumbers.TelephoneNumbers(1 To
                                       dcTelephoneNumbers.Count)

         For intDocument = 1 To dcTelephoneNumbers.Count
         Set docTelephoneNumber =
                     dcTelephoneNumbers.GetNthDocument(intDocument)
         TelephoneNumbers.TelephoneNumbers(intDocument) =
              docTelephoneNumber.GetItemValue("TelephoneNumber")(0)
         Next

       Else
         Redim TelephoneNumbers.TelephoneNumbers(1 To 1)
         TelephoneNumbers.TelephoneNumbers(1) =
                                   "No Telephone Numbers Available"
       End If

       Set GetTelephoneNumbers = TelephoneNumbers

  End Function

  Function GetAddress(strSymbol As String, FAULT As WS_FAULT)
                                                    As AddressInfo

     Dim dbCurrent As NotesDatabase
     Dim viewAddressLookup As NotesView
     Dim docAddress As NotesDocument
     Dim Address As AddressInfo

     Set dbCurrent = session.CurrentDatabase
     Set viewAddressLookup = dbCurrent.GetView("AddressLookup")
     Set docAddress = viewAddressLookup.GetDocumentByKey(strSymbol)
     Set Address = New AddressInfo()
```

```
    If docAddress Is Nothing Then
      Address.Street = "None Available"
      Address.City = "None Available"
      Address.State = "None Available"
      Address.Zip = 0
    Else
      Address.Street = docAddress.GetItemValue("Street")(0)
      Address.City = docAddress.GetItemValue("City")(0)
      Address.State = docAddress.GetItemValue("State")(0)
      Address.Zip = docAddress.GetItemValue("Zip")(0)
    End If

    Set GetAddress = Address

  End Function

  Function GetShortInterest(strSymbol As String, FAULT As WS_FAULT)
                                                            As Long
    Dim dbCurrent As NotesDatabase
    Dim viewCompanyProfileLookup As NotesView
    Dim docCompanyProfile As NotesDocument

    Set dbCurrent = session.CurrentDatabase
    Set viewCompanyProfileLookup =
                      dbCurrent.GetView("CompanyProfileLookup")
    Set docCompanyProfile =
            viewCompanyProfileLookup.GetDocumentByKey(strSymbol)

    If (docCompanyProfile Is Nothing) Then
      ' *** no match found
      FAULT.setFault(True)
      Call FAULT.setFaultString("No match found for " & strSymbol)
    Else
      GetShortInterest =
              docCompanyProfile.GetItemValue("ShortInterest")(0)
    End If
  End Function
End Class
```

We can now use the Web Services Explorer to browse the new GetAddress function and review the results of returning a complex data type:

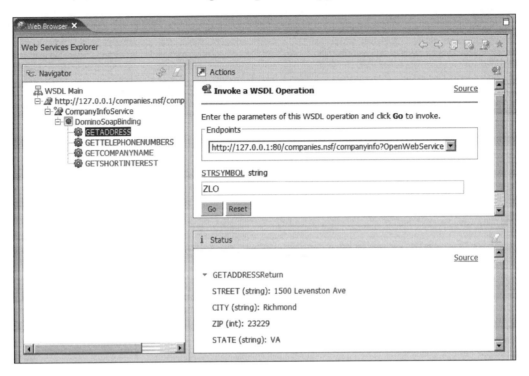

Notice in the bottom right panel that each AddressInfo member variable returned by the GetAddress function is enumerated by name and type. This data was returned as a single response and contains multiple data types. This provides a means to upload related data into a single response.

Now that we have a functional web service returning a variety of data formats using LotusScript, let us now turn our attention towards a Java-based implementation of this service.

Implementing the CompanyInfo Web Service Using Java

Java's popularity has grown tremendously in recent years. It is a frequent choice for web-services implementations. Java contains a number of utility classes that are easily combined with Domino-based design idioms. We will now look at how to implement the CompanyInfo web service using Java. The following Java code approximates the LotusScript implementation of a simple web service.

```
import lotus.domino.*;
import lotus.domino.types.*;

public class CompanyInfo {

   Session session;

      public CompanyInfo() {
         session = WebServiceBase.getCurrentSession();
      }

      public String getCompanyName(String strSymbol) {

         String strCompanyName = new String();

          try {
             AgentContext agentContext = session.getAgentContext();
             Database dbCurrent = agentContext.getCurrentDatabase();
             View viewCompanyProfileLookup =
                         dbCurrent.getView("CompanyProfileLookup");
             Document docCompanyProfile =
                   viewCompanyProfileLookup.getDocumentByKey(strSymbol,
                                                            false);
             if (docCompanyProfile != null) {
                strCompanyName =
                       docCompanyProfile.getItemValueString("Company");
             } else {
                strCompanyName = "No Company found for " + strSymbol;
                }
          } catch(Exception e) {
             e.printStackTrace();
             }
      return strCompanyName;
   }
}
```

This code returns a string indicating the Company Name for the supplied ticker symbol. Let's continue to examine how we might return a string array using Java. In Java, it is possible to return a string array directly from the service operation. There is no need to define an additional class for this:

```
import lotus.domino.*;
import lotus.domino.types.*;

public class CompanyInfo {

   Session session;
```

```java
public CompanyInfo() {
  session = WebServiceBase.getCurrentSession();
}

public String getCompanyName(String strSymbol) {

  String strCompanyName = new String();

  try {
    AgentContext agentContext = session.getAgentContext();
    Database dbCurrent = agentContext.getCurrentDatabase();
    View viewCompanyProfileLookup =
              dbCurrent.getView("CompanyProfileLookup");
    Document docCompanyProfile =
        viewCompanyProfileLookup.getDocumentByKey(strSymbol,
                                                      false);

    if (docCompanyProfile != null) {
      strCompanyName =
            docCompanyProfile.getItemValueString("Company");
    } else {
        strCompanyName = "No Company Found for " + strSymbol;
      }
  } catch(Exception e) {
      e.printStackTrace();
    }
    return strCompanyName;
}

public String[] getTelephoneNumbers(String strSymbol) {

  String[] saTelephoneNumbers;
  saTelephoneNumbers = new String[1];

  try {
    AgentContext agentContext =  session.getAgentContext();
    Database dbCurrent = agentContext.getCurrentDatabase();
    View viewTelephoneNumberLookup =
              dbCurrent.getView("TelephoneNumbersLookup");
    DocumentCollection dcTelephoneNumbers =
    viewTelephoneNumberLookup.getAllDocumentsByKey(strSymbol,
                                                      false);
```

```
    if (dcTelephoneNumbers.getCount() > 0) {
      saTelephoneNumbers =
                    new String[dcTelephoneNumbers.getCount()];
      for (int intX = 0; intX < dcTelephoneNumbers.getCount() ;
                                                    intX++) {
        Document docTelephoneNumber =
                    dcTelephoneNumbers.getNthDocument(intX + 1);
        saTelephoneNumbers[intX] =
          docTelephoneNumber.getItemValueString("TelephoneNumber");
      }
    } else {
      saTelephoneNumbers = new String[1];
      saTelephoneNumbers[0] = "No match found for " + strSymbol;
      return saTelephoneNumbers;
      }
  } catch(Exception e) {
    e.printStackTrace();
    }
  return saTelephoneNumbers;
  }
}
```

Let's continue to expand our Java implementation of the `CompanyInfo` web service by adding the `GetAddress(String, strSymbol)` method. This operation will return a class instance containing multiple data types. In a similar fashion to the LotusScript implementation, we will return three strings and an integer as a single response.

To implement this code, we must use the **New Class** button to add the class definition. If you add the class by manually typing it before or after the `CompanyInfo` class definition, you will get compile-time errors. This button is highlighted in the screenshot that follows. Also notice that **AddressInfo.java** is generated by the Domino Designer 7 Java editor as a result of the class addition. Domino Designer 7 provides a horizontal gray separator bar that identifies a new class definition separate from the primary `PortType` class that handles web-service clients' requests.

Use the **New Class** design action to add the `AddressInfo` class. Typing it directly into the editor before or after the `CompanyInfo` class generates an error.

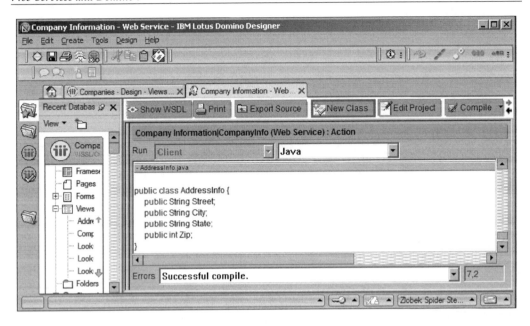

To complete the Java implementation corresponding to the previous LotusScript example, we will also add a getShortInterest operation. The following Java code completes the Java implementation of the previous LotusScript example:

```java
import lotus.domino.*;
import lotus.domino.types.*;

public class CompanyInfo {

  Session session;

  public CompanyInfo() {
    session = WebServiceBase.getCurrentSession();
  }

  public String getCompanyName(String strSymbol) {

    String strCompanyName = new String();

    try {
      AgentContext agentContext = session.getAgentContext();
      Database dbCurrent = agentContext.getCurrentDatabase();
      View viewCompanyProfileLookup =
                dbCurrent.getView("CompanyProfileLookup");
      Document docCompanyProfile =
      viewCompanyProfileLookup.getDocumentByKey(strSymbol, false);
if (docCompanyProfile != null) {
        strCompanyName =
```

```
                    docCompanyProfile.getItemValueString("Company");
    } else {
      strCompanyName = "No Company Found for " + strSymbol;
      }
  } catch(Exception e) {
    e.printStackTrace();
    }
    return strCompanyName;
}

public String[] getTelephoneNumbers(String strSymbol) {

  String[] saTelephoneNumbers;
  saTelephoneNumbers = new String[1];

  try {
    AgentContext agentContext = session.getAgentContext();
    Database dbCurrent = agentContext.getCurrentDatabase();
    View viewTelephoneNumberLookup =
              dbCurrent.getView("TelephoneNumbersLookup");
    DocumentCollection dcTelephoneNumbers =
    viewTelephoneNumberLookup.getAllDocumentsByKey(strSymbol,
                                                   false);

    if (dcTelephoneNumbers.getCount() > 0) {
      saTelephoneNumbers =
                   new String[dcTelephoneNumbers.getCount()];
      for (int intX = 0; intX < dcTelephoneNumbers.getCount() ;
                                                   intX++) {
        Document docTelephoneNumber =
                dcTelephoneNumbers.getNthDocument(intX + 1);
        saTelephoneNumbers[intX] =
          docTelephoneNumber.getItemValueString("TelephoneNumber");
      }
    } else {
      saTelephoneNumbers = new String[1];
      saTelephoneNumbers[0] = "No match found for " + strSymbol;
      return saTelephoneNumbers;
      }
  } catch(Exception e) {
    e.printStackTrace();
    }
  return saTelephoneNumbers;   }

public AddressInfo getAddress(String strSymbol) {
  AddressInfo Address = new AddressInfo();
  System.out.println("1");
```

```
    try {
          System.out.println("2");
          AgentContext agentContext = session.getAgentContext();
          Database dbCurrent = agentContext.getCurrentDatabase();
          View viewAddressLookup =
                              dbCurrent.getView("AddressLookup");
          Document docAddress =
             viewAddressLookup.getDocumentByKey(strSymbol, false);
          System.out.println("3");
          if (docAddress != null) {
            System.out.println("4");
            Address.Street = docAddress.getItemValueString("Street");
            System.out.println("5");
            Address.City = docAddress.getItemValueString("City");
            System.out.println("6");
            Address.State = docAddress.getItemValueString("State");
            System.out.println("7");
            Address.Zip = docAddress.getItemValueInteger("Zip");
            System.out.println("8");
          } else {
      }
    } catch(Exception e) {
      }
return Address;
}

public long getShortInterest(String strSymbol) {

  long lngShortInterest = 0;

  try {
    AgentContext agentContext =  session.getAgentContext();
    Database dbCurrent = agentContext.getCurrentDatabase();
    View viewCompanyProfileLookup =
                  dbCurrent.getView("CompanyProfileLookup");
    Document docCompanyProfile =
    viewCompanyProfileLookup.getDocumentByKey(strSymbol, false);
    if (docCompanyProfile != null) {
      lngShortInterest=
          docCompanyProfile.getItemValueInteger("ShortInterest");
  } else {
      lngShortInterest = -1;
      }
  } catch(Exception e) {
    e.printStackTrace();
      }
```

```
            return lngShortInterest;
    }
}

public class AddressInfo {
    public String Street;
    public String City;
    public String State;
    public int Zip;
}
```

We can now browse the new Java operations using the Web Services Explorer. The Web Services Explorer does not distinguish between a Java and LotusScript based web service. One interesting thing to note, however, is that Domino 7 returns the Address object's member elements in a different order from LotusScript. This is based on the format of the SOAP response generated by Domino. This does not have a functional impact on the data returned to the web-service client. The following screenshot shows the complex data type returned by the getAddress(String strSymbol) operation:

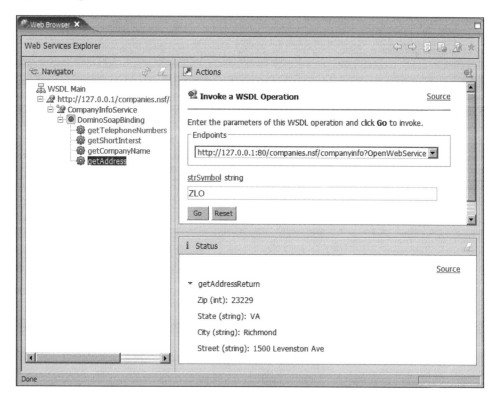

We have implemented simple and complex web services using both LotusScript and Java. We will now finish our examination of Domino 7 based web services by reviewing the actions provided by Domino Designer 7 to interact with the WSDL it generates.

Domino Designer WSDL Actions

Domino Designer 7's web-service design editor provides several action buttons that are useful for basic WSDL actions. These are highlighted in the following screenshot, followed by a description of their function.

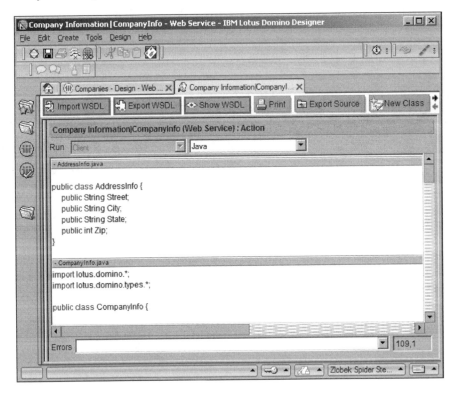

Export WSDL

This button is used to auto-generate a WSDL file that describes the interface for the selected web service. The button prompts you for a file export location and then exports a WSDL document describing the operations defined by the web service. The information exported by this action is the same information generated by the `?openwebservice` URL that has the format:

```
http://servername/database.nsf/webservicename?openwebservice
```

The **Export WSDL** action is particularly useful for sharing a web-service interface definition in cases where the web-service consumer does not yet have direct HTTP access to the Domino server.

Import WSDL

The **Import WSDL** design action is used to begin a new web service based on an existing interface definition. This action assumes that the web-service interface has already been designed. Clicking this button prompts the developer for a WSDL file and then generates a skeletal web-service implementation that defines the operations specified in WSDL. You are then free to complete the implementation of the defined interface. The skeletal implementation is either Java or LotusScript, based on the language you specify. One useful application of this is for architects to specify web-service operations using WSDL, and then hand off the implementation to developers.

To illustrate the use of these two buttons, we will export the WSDL for our CompanyInfo web service and then import it back into an empty web service. Doing so in LotusScript results in stubbed service operations similar to the following screenshot:

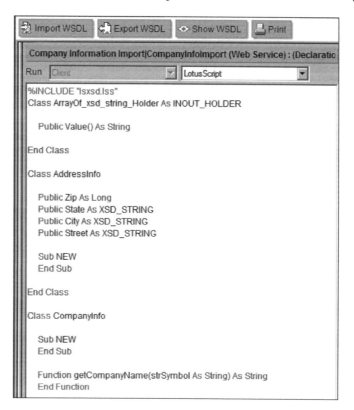

We can also do the same when selecting Java. Importing WSDL into a Java-based web service generates a skeletal implementation as seen in the following:

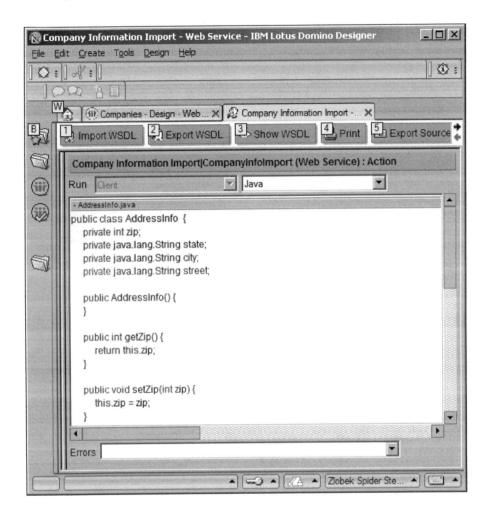

Show WSDL

Show WSDL opens a browser and dynamically outputs a WSDL document describing the web-service's interface. This is similar to opening the following Domino-based URL pattern:

```
http://servername/database.nsf/webservicename?openwebservice
```

UDDI Registries

A UDDI registry provides an exchange for web services. Its purpose is to facilitate the discovery and consumption of web services among different parties that typically are not directly familiar with each other. Each UDDI registry can have its own terms and conditions. Some may require authentication to access free web services. Others may allow publishers to sell their services to third-party consumers. UDDI registries are not a requirement for you to publish and consume web services, but provide a venue for you to either locate a particular web service that you might need without developing it yourself, or to publish your web service for a target audience.

The following screenshot shows the Web Services Explorer accessing **the IBM UDDI Test Registry**. This registry is one that requires a user name and password:

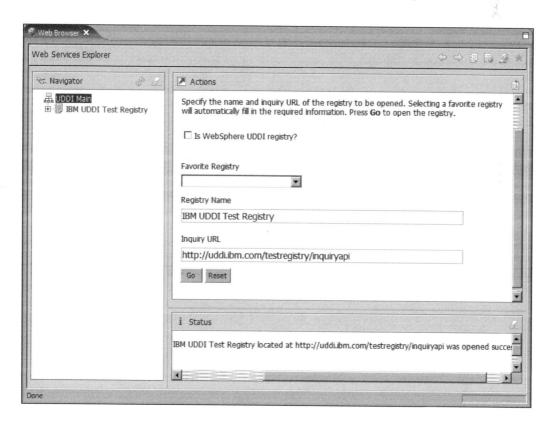

Summary

This chapter examined web-service features and their Domino-based implementations. We examined web services that returned both simple and complex data types. We further examined this in both LotusScript and Java. We also looked at the various tools Domino Designer 7 provides for interacting with WSDL. We finished by examining the role UDDI plays in facilitating the adoption of web services.

9

Optimizing Application Performance

For many years, we, the authors, worked in the support organization at Lotus (and then IBM), helping customers troubleshoot and work around their performance problems. Most often, we found that if the customer had had a bit more knowledge about coding for performance and understood a little better how Domino works, they could have avoided their performance problems entirely.

In this chapter, we will cover three areas that significantly impact on your applications: database properties, views, and forms/agents.

Database Properties

In this section, we look into two database properties of particular interest to performance—Unread Marks and Optimize Document Table Map.

Unread Marks

In real-world installations, there is a substantial penalty in large databases for having Unread Marks enabled. So if your application doesn't use them, turn this feature off at the database level. To do this, open the database and select **File | Database | Properties**, then open the last (beanie) tab, and select the **Don't maintain unread marks** option.

Following is an example (somewhat cleaned up for easier reading) of the output you might see if you ran your client debugger while opening a database:

```
GET_UNREAD_NOTE_TABLE: 600 ms
OPEN_COLLECTION(REP85256055:004781F8-NTFFFF0020,0040,0000)
OPEN_DB(CN=HQ/OU=Boston/O=Acme!!Applications\SalesTracking.nsf):
(Connect to HQ/Boston/Acme: 5000 ms)
GET_UNREAD_NOTE_TABLE: 4000 ms
RCV_UNREAD 2000 ms
```

All the preceding lines appear if Unread Marks is enabled. However, only the highlighted lines appear if Unread Marks is disabled. This gives you some indication of how much less processing needs to be performed for some tasks when Unread Marks is disabled. This is just an example; your experience might well be different. But it helps demonstrate the significance of this setting.

In practice, a large application might take about 5 seconds for a user to open with Unread Marks disabled, and over 11 seconds with Unread Marks enabled—a very substantial difference!

Optimize Document Table Map

This option is designed to help index views faster in your Domino Directory. However, in the first releases of Notes/Domino 7, this setting does not appear to enhance performance. Testing appears to indicate a slight degradation in performance with this setting enabled. A bug report has been sent to Lotus/IBM and at some point in the future, this will presumably be working as designed.

Views

View performance has always been less well-understood than some other areas of performance tuning, probably because it appears to be so much more difficult to measure and do something about. We have performed extensive tests over the years, and have found that there are some tips and techniques that can help you optimize view performance for your application and the underlying server.

The first thing you should do to understand view performance is to familiarize yourself with how views get built and maintained (indexed). The Domino server has a task called **Update** that maintains view indexes. It runs every 15 minutes by default, and will process every view in every database on the server, provided that the database has had some user (or mail, or replication) activity since the Update task last ran. On very efficient application servers, you should see the Update task finish in less than a minute, thus preserving the bulk of the Domino server's resources during the next 14 minutes for addressing user requests. At busy times or on busy servers, this indexing time will creep up. If it requires full 15 minutes to index all the databases on the server, the server is in a bad state. This is because the indexer will be running constantly throughout the day, consuming resources that would otherwise be directly responding to user requests.

Except for some unusual cases, you probably won't change how *often* your data gets updated. What you can change, however, is how *long* it takes to update the views in your applications. The rest of this section will be devoted to understanding some features which impact on the Update task's ability to quickly index your views, and what to do about it.

 If you want to see how long it takes to update views on your server (which is a great idea), go to Chapter 11, *Troubleshooting Application*, for tips on how to do this.

Reducing View Size

Typically, on any server, the bigger databases with more documents and more views take longer to update. That's not a big surprise. What might be a surprise, though, is that the document size is irrelevant. What is relevant is the amount of data that is displayed in views. So if you have many columns or columns that display large text fields and are truncated only by the limitation of the user's screen, these views could be easily spruced up by simply reducing the number of columns and by using a simple formula such as:

```
@Left(BigTextField; 40)
```

For a nicer look, we suggest writing such formulas in this way:

```
Btf := BigTextField;
Len := @Length(Btf);
@If(Len < 40; Btf; @LeftBack(@Left(Btf; 40); " ") + " …")
```

This will truncate your column between words and append ellipses to the end, which is more pleasing than truncating in the middle of a word.

Categorized Columns

A commonly used feature that causes significant delays in indexing is categorizing columns. The more columns categorized in a view, the larger and slower that view will be. The effect can be quite dramatic, with each additional categorized column (that is, making a sorted column into a categorized column) increasing the time to index the view.

For example, if your view takes *n* seconds to index with five columns, the first four of which are sorted, then it might take *n* times two seconds if you make the first column categorized, *n* times three seconds if there are two categorized columns, and so on. This is not a hard-and-fast rule, because the performance impact greatly depends upon how the data breaks down when categorized. A view in your mail file categorized on the **SendTo** field, for example, would become very large and slow compared to one which was categorized on the **From** field.

If your application is a web application, then an effective solution for many view problems is to embed your views and use Show Single Category. Even if that requires you to make the view larger and more complex, it will display very quickly and efficiently for users. See the *Reader Names* section later in this chapter for even more reasons to use this kind of a view.

Time/Date

Very useful (but poorly performing) views are ones that use time/date sensitive formulas—@Today or @Now in the view selection formula or a column formula. Typically, you would use this type of view to:

- Display only documents that are overdue
- Display a special icon next to documents that are overdue

Unfortunately, each time a user opens a time/date sensitive view, it forces the server to refresh the view entirely from scratch (that is, rebuild it), which is time consuming. Roughly speaking, such a view takes more than 100 times as long to refresh as a comparably sized non-time/date sensitive view.

There are many ways to avoid this situation. You could run an agent nightly that marks overdue documents in such a way that your view can display them appropriately. You could simply display all documents and show/sort on their due date. Or, if you really want to keep the time/date sensitive view as is, you could change the indexing options so that it refreshes only when explicitly requested by a user clicking the refresh arrow (top-left corner of the view) or the *F9* key. This is done by setting the indexing option to **Manual**.

Another variation would be to open the **View** properties and set the indexing options to **Auto, at most every**, and then select an appropriate minimum indexing interval.

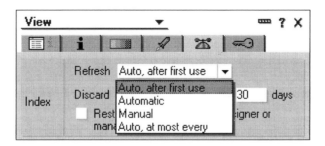

If, for example, you chose two hours, then users can go in and out of that view for two hours without worrying about it refreshing (rebuilding), but after two hours the next user (and the server!) would be hit with that delay. Keep in mind that the reason the view is very responsive during this two-hour period is because it is not updating. So it is possible that your data is getting stale. For some applications, this is an acceptable risk/drawback, but not for other applications.

And of course, at any time, a user can click on the reload arrow or their *F9* key to force the view to refresh (rebuild) immediately.

Reader Names

The final piece of the view puzzle is Reader Names. Reader Names are frequently used in documents to provide excellent security against unauthorized access to that data. The downside can be most easily seen in large databases that have many users with limited access to the data. For example, suppose you have a Sales Tracking application with 100,000 documents and a few thousand users. Suppose further that your users have access in a pyramid fashion:

- Executive Management team has access to all documents.
- Regional Managers have access to their region's data, say 25% of the total.
- District Managers have access to their district's data, say 1%.
- Managers have access to the data for their sales representatives, say 0.1%.
- Finally, each individual sales representative has access to his or her own data, say 0.01%.

There might be 5 or 10 people at the top, and many thousands at the bottom (thus the "pyramid"). When each individual user tries to access the database, the user's ability to see each document has to be verified by the server, which can be time-consuming.

Roughly speaking, what happens is that when you open a view, the server has to fill your screen with information. This is approximately 50 rows of data, with a lot of leeway for different resolutions, multiple rows per document, and so on.

If you have access to the first 50 documents, then this is easy. But if you have access to only half the data in the view, then the server will have to work approximately twice as long to get enough data to display for you (statistically, because you might coincidentally have access to more or fewer documents that happen to be at the top of the view). If you have access to only 0.01%, then the server will have to work 10,000 times as long! You can imagine that if there were even a small number of users trying to access a large view simultaneously, this might be quite a burden on the server.

Here are some ways to mitigate this kind of problem:

- **Reader Names**: Don't use Readers Names; we would never suggest making an insecure application, but we have seen many applications that use Reader Names fields that are not in fact protecting against security threats of any kind. So verify that you have this need before utilizing Reader Names fields on your data.

- **Embedded view using Show Single Category**: From extensive tests, we have seen that users can get results back faster this way than when they open the native view with no Reader Names fields on any documents. The only downside to this approach is that the Notes-client interface, using embedded views, is not as seamless as the web-browser interface. So if your application is for Notes users, you may decide that this isn't a satisfactory solution. Also, you will need to have a reasonable set of categories to base the Show Single Category formula on. For most applications, this is not a problem, but it may require some thought.

- **Local replicas**: In the example of our Sales Tracking application, the individual sales representatives might reasonably have local replicas of just their own data, which would then be very fast to access. Maintaining local replicas brings its own set of challenges, but it does solve a lot of problems with regard to performance and constant access to data.

- **Categorizing the view**: This sounds overly simple, and yet it works very well. If the default view is categorized simply, for instance by Sales rep name, and the view is collapsed by default, then the view will open very fast for all users. To get to your documents, you would have to click the twistie next to your name to expand that category, but since you'd have access to all the documents in that category, that would also be fast.

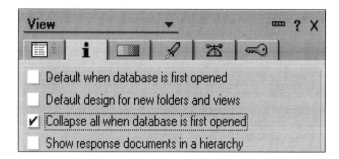

Forms and Agents

We have saved the most obvious for last. And why are forms and agents the most obvious place to look at performance? Because forms are what users spend most of their time working with, and agents leave a distinct trail that can be monitored and analyzed. What makes this section worthy of an entire book in its own right is that you can use so many programming languages in forms and agents, and you can write virtually unlimited quantities of code. So to speak of optimizing performance in forms and agents is to discuss the topic of generally good programming practices.

In this section, we'll cover some of the most important parts of your form or agent code in terms of performance. We'll look at common performance errors and how to address them. We hope these examples illustrate principles that can be applied to many more situations in your applications. Fortunately, our years of experience developing applications and troubleshooting for performance problems has shown that these kinds of problems are often not hard to address.

Domino Objects are Expensive

When you need to iterate through all the views in a database, or all the fields in a document, you might think of writing your code this way:

```
Forall v in db.views
Print v.name   ' or whatever real code you have
End Forall
```

Instead, it's far better to write it this way:

```
vViews = db.views
Forall v in vViews
    Print v.name   ' or whatever real code you have
End Forall
```

The reason is simply that storing database views in a variable will allow your code to loop (in the `Forall`) without repeatedly referencing the database object itself. Databases can be big, they can be far away, and there is no reason to force your code to conduct that conversation more than once.

Similarly, if you are working with a single item on a document, you might want to write it in this way:

```
Set Doc = uidoc.document   ' current document
Doc.Field1 = Doc.Amount ( 0 ) + 100
Doc.Field2 = Doc.Amount ( 0 ) * .15
Doc.Field3 = Doc.Amount ( 0 ) * .0585
Doc.Field4 = Doc.Amount ( 0 ) + 85
```

But, as in the preceding example, it would be better to store `Doc.Amount` in a temporary variable, like this:

```
Set Doc = uidoc.document   ' current document
Dim Amount as Double
Amount = Doc.Amount ( 0 )
Doc.Field1 = Amount + 100
Doc.Field2 = Amount * .15
Doc.Field3 = Amount * .0585
Doc.Field4 = Amount + 85
```

This is true even if the document is sitting in Edit mode in your client, because the field references are against a copy of the document, which is time-consuming to check.

Search Methods

If your code needs to get a handle to one or more documents, you have multiple methods available to access those documents. Some of these include:

```
Db.search
Db.ftsearch
View.GetAllDocumentsByKey
```

It turns out that certain methods tend to be more efficient than others. This is certainly true for differently sized databases and document collections (how many documents you get). The rough rule to use is that `view.GetAllDocumentsByKey` and `db.ftsearch` are almost always the fastest methods. This is particularly true for small collections of documents and large databases.

Saving Documents

A good rule to keep in mind is that saving a document is time-consuming. For example, suppose you have some code that iterates through many documents updating fields in each document and then saving them, but sometimes a document is already updated. Something like this might be one approach:

```
' Assume some kind of loop through a collection of documents
doc.Field1 = f1
doc.Field2 = f2
doc.Field3 = f3
call doc.save ( false, false )
```

Instead, consider the following code:

```
Tf1$ = doc.Field1 ( 0 )
Tf2$ = doc.Field2 ( 0 )
Tf3$ = doc.Field3 ( 0 )
MustUpdate$ = "Yes"
If Tf1$ = f1 then
    If Tf2$ = f2 then
      If Tf3$ = f3 then
          MustUpdate$ = "No"
      End If
    End If
End If

If MustUpdate$ = "Yes" then
doc.Field1 = f1
doc.Field2 = f2
doc.Field3 = f3
Call doc.save ( false, false )
End if
```

Without question, this is more cumbersome code to write, especially if there are many fields of varying data types, some are multi-value, and so on. But the underlying truth is that the checking portion of the code will run very fast, and the document save will run comparably slowly. So it's better to write the code that carefully checks whether you need to save.

Keyword @Db Formulas

This is a prevalent feature of sophisticated applications, and unfortunately it's often a performance killer. There are a few related problems that can arise in the following situations:

- You want the latest and greatest data from some lookup, for example company names.
- You might have a handful of lookups that are related to one another. So once you have chosen a company, you might get a company-specific list of customer names, products, or addresses.

The only problem that you or your users see is that the document draws very slowly, even in the Read mode.

The way to handle this kind of functionality is to first consider how often users create, edit, and read these documents. And when they create and edit the documents, do they use the drop-down lists frequently or infrequently?

If it turns out that these are infrequently used compared to the total number of edits in the document, then it's probably best to offload them to a dialog box or pop up, and have a button next to each computed field (actually, make them **Computed when composed**). The button calls the dialog box or pop-up window, and then pushes the selected value into the **Computed when composed** field. The field performs no work, and is therefore very fast. The only slowdown occurs when a user deliberately presses the button.

This solution works very well for documents which have many sections and only some of which are used at any one time. It also works well for documents that receive frequent edits but not edits to these keyword drop-down fields.

If, on the other hand, your documents are not edited frequently, or if these keyword drop-down fields are among the frequently edited fields when the document is edited, then it's impractical from a usability perspective to have buttons and dialog boxes. Instead, use regular keyword fields and write a formula such as this:

```
@If(@IsDocBeingEdited; ""; @Return(KeywordFieldName));
@DbColumn("Notes"; ""; "ViewName"; 1)
```

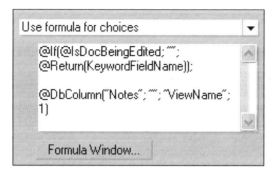

This prevents the @Db formula from computing if the document is in Read mode, which is very helpful for performance. It also feels intuitively correct to not burden users with the lookup if they are only in Read mode. However, if you do this, you will also want to put a line of code into your PostModeChange event, to make sure that users who switch from Read to Edit mode get the benefit of fresh lookups:

```
If source.EditMode Then Call source.Refresh
```

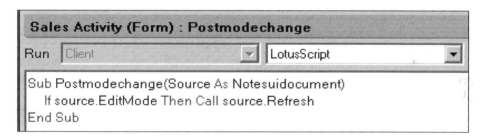

You will also need to select the **Refresh choices on document refresh** option in your keyword fields.

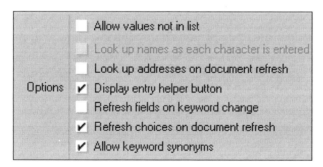

Finally, a very helpful feature for optimizing performance of @Db formulas is to consider a view that uses **Generate unique keys in index**.

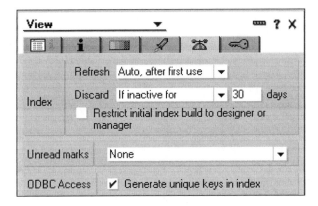

This is not feasible for all views and data, but the following is an example where it would be very helpful. Suppose your Sales Tracking database has approximately 100 companies, each of which has on an average 1,000 sales records. If you want to have a keyword field that allows you to choose the company name from a list, and you get this list by performing a lookup against a view of sales records, you might write the code in this way:

```
@Unique(@DbColumn("Notes"; ""; "(Lookup-SalesRecordsByCompany)"; 1)
```

But if you took that view and enabled the **Generate unique keys in index** option, then it would perform the same function as your @Unique. The point here is that instead of your view having 100,000 documents, it would have only 100 documents. That means faster indexing, faster @Db lookup formula, and better performance for your users.

There are a couple of caveats to using this feature in views:

- The view should be dispensed with the other data, so if you want to get all the documents for a specific company, for instance, then this would be a bad view to use.

- If your key is multi-value, then you may need to code a workaround to avoid missing values. This is no big deal; you can simply write something like this in your view column:

```
@Implode(MultiValueField; "~")
```

Then, in your @DbColumn formula, you will want to explode the returned list, like this:

```
@Unique(@Explode(@DbColumn("Notes"; "";
      "(Lookup-SalesRecordsByCompany)"; 1); "~"))
```

You include @Unique because after you've exploded the list, it is possible that duplicate values will be found.

Summary

We hope this chapter has introduced, or reinforced, some good practices in terms of optimizing your applications for performance. We have rarely seen an application that could not be efficiently coded to work well in a Domino environment. Much more often, the application has simply not been coded with performance in mind, and there are agents, views, forms, and even database properties that are inefficiently configured for your application to be as fast as it can be.

See Chapter 11, *Troubleshooting Applications*, for tips on how to determine whether your code is executing too slowly.

10
Code Samples

This chapter describes sample code that uses some of the new programming features offered in Lotus Notes/Domino 7. You can download a Domino database containing this code from here: `http://www.packtpub.com/support`. These code samples illustrate a number of interesting features in release 7 while offering some practical examples you may be interested in incorporating into your own applications.

The samples we provide include the following features:

- Save & Close action bar button
- Preventing editing of fields and documents dynamically
- Fast DBLookups
- InViewEditing

The sample Domino database that accompanies this chapter contains examples of these features "in action".

The Save & Close Action Bar Button

Most **Save & Close** buttons don't account for `QuerySave` events or field validation formulas that might find invalid data and stop the save. You can tell you have such a button when it asks you a second time if you want to save the document, even after a pop up has told you that you've entered some data incorrectly or left a field blank.

The fix is easy. Make your **Save & Close** button LotusScript, and just write code similar to the following into the `Click` event:

```
On Error Goto oopsie  ' in this case, this will simply stop execution
Dim w As New NotesUIWorkspace
Dim uidoc As NotesUIDocument
Set uidoc = w.CurrentDocument
```

```
Call uidoc.save
Call uidoc.close
Exit Sub

oopsie:
    Exit Sub
```

Now if the `QuerySave` event or validation formulas trap an error, your code will simply stop execution after the `call uidoc.save` line, so it won't execute the `call uidoc.close` line. This may seem like a lot of work to simply stop an extra pop up from annoying users, but in this popup-happy world, many users will appreciate it.

The Appointment form in the sample database contains an example of the **Save & Close** action bar button.

Preventing Editing of Fields and Documents Dynamically

Another common situation is one where some (or all) users need to be prevented from being able to edit documents but these users are still allowed to see the documents. Although you can use AuthorNames fields in many situations, this means that users have Author access in the ACL (Access Control List), sometimes more access is required for an application.

An example might be an application where users are allowed to make certain document edits (for instance, from the view using InViewEdit), but otherwise should be restricted from editing documents. By using the `PostOpen` and `QueryModeChange` events, you can prevent users from entering into Edit mode, with the following message box appearing:

The code for this is as follows:

```
Sub Postopen(Source As Notesuidocument)
    If source.EditMode Then
       Dim doc As notesdocument
```

```
         Set doc = source.Document
            If doc.EditAllow ( 0 ) = "0" Then
               Messagebox "You are not allowed to edit this document.",
               64, "Information"
               source.EditMode = False
               Exit Sub
            End If
         End If
End Sub

Sub Querymodechange(Source As Notesuidocument, Continue As Variant)
      If Not ( source.EditMode ) Then
         Dim doc As notesdocument
         Set doc = source.Document
            If doc.EditAllow ( 0 ) = "0" Then
               Messagebox "You are not allowed to edit this document.",
               64, "Information"
                  Continue = False
                  Exit Sub
            End If
      End If
End Sub
```

The logic for these events is as follows:

- **PostOpen**: If the document is being opened in Edit mode, then check the EditAllow field to see if the user is allowed to edit this document. If not, pop up the message box and switch back to Read mode.

- **QueryModeChange**: If the document is currently in Read mode, then check the EditAllow field to see if the user is allowed to edit this document. If not, pop up the message box and stop the code from continuing. (`Continue = False` will prevent the document from switching to Edit mode.)

Notes/Domino 7 has upgraded another related feature, the InputEnabled field event. In release 6, this allowed you to deny editing of a field if the field used Native OS Style, but not if it used Notes Style. In Notes/Domino 7, this feature works for both types of fields. Using an @ formula, you simply write code that results in `@True (1)` or `@False (0)`. If False, the field is not editable. If `True`, then it is editable. You can compute field values and user roles, perform @Db formulas, and so on. For example, in the Appointment form in our sample Domino database, the SalesRep field has the following formula in its InputEnabled field event:

```
@If(@IsMember("[Admin]"; @UserRoles); @True; @False)
```

This means that anyone with the `[Admin]` role can edit this field, but others cannot.

Note that neither of these methods of preventing the editing of fields is truly secure, because users can still use agents, for example, to modify the data using the back-end document.

The Appointment form in the sample database contains an example of preventing the editing of fields and documents dynamically.

Fast DbLookups

During our many years of examining applications for performance problems, @DbLookups have popped up more often than we can count. The usefulness of this functionality is undeniable, but so too can be the slowdowns incurred when an application form needs several lookups to large views. Even worse, these @Db formulas often execute even when the document is opened in Read mode. Note that for web applications, drop-down lists will not execute their @Db formulas in Read mode, but for Notes client applications, they will (at least by default).

The following steps can dramatically improve the performance of @Db formulas in keyword fields, regardless of whether the application is for web browsers or Notes clients:

1. Create a keyword drop-down field
2. Use `PostModeChange` event to refresh the keyword list
3. Create a view for the lookup

The following sections describe these three steps in detail.

Creating Keyword Drop-Down Fields

The first step is to create your keyword drop-down field. In the Appointment form in our sample Domino database, we include such a field, called *Categories*.

- Keyword field: `Categories`
- Keyword formula:

```
@If(@IsDocBeingEdited; ""; @Return(Categories));
list := @DbColumn("Notes"; ""; "(Lookup-Categories)"; 1);
@Unique(list) if you are using Notes/Domino 7 applications
                and servers
@Unique(@Explode(list; "~")) if you might have replica copies
                on Notes/Domino 6 servers
```

This code does the following: If the document is in Read mode, it simply returns the value that has already been chosen. If the document is in Edit mode, it performs the lookup. See the *Creating a View for the Lookup* section, described later in this chapter for an explanation on why the longer formula is necessary in Notes/Domino 6.

- Keyword options: **Refresh choices on document refresh** (mandatory) and **Allow values not in list** (optional). See the description for the PostModeChange event below for further explanation.

Using the PostModeChange Event to Refresh the Keyword List

The second step is to use the PostModeChange event to refresh the keyword list if the document switches from Read mode to Edit mode.

```
PostModeChange Event:
Sub Postmodechange(Source As Notesuidocument)
    If source.EditMode Then source.Refresh
End Sub
```

If the document is opened in Edit mode, then all drop-down lists will execute normally (@IsDocBeingEdited...). However, if the document is opened in Read mode, and then the user switches to Edit mode, there is no native automatic refresh and so we have to explicitly request this refresh.

Creating a View for the Lookup

The third step is to create a view for the lookup. In our sample database, the (Lookup-Categories) view has a single column that references the field Categories.

This view has a special feature enabled **Generate unique keys in index**. This feature eliminates all duplicate entries from the view, as determined by what is displayed in the view columns. Since we have only a single column displaying the Categories field, we could easily have hundreds or thousands of duplicate documents. By eliminating them from the view index, we greatly speed up the view indexing, and therefore @Db lookups, as well.

If your Categories field is single value, then you can simply reference that field in the single column in this view, sort that column, have your Keyword field reference this view using @DbColumn, and you're all set. But if the Categories field is multi-value, then you have to do a bit more work.

For Notes/Domino 7, all you have to do is turn on **Show multiple values as separate entries** in the view column, and then in your keyword formula use `@Unique(@DbColumn(...))`. `@Unique` is required because there are cases where duplicate values will be displayed in the view, even after using this Unique Keys feature.

For Notes/Domino 6, however, you will find that using **Show multiple values as separate entries** may not preserve every value in your view. (See the example below.) In order to preserve all values, use this as your column formula:

```
@Implode(Categories; "~")
```

This will almost certainly introduce some duplicate entries, so your keyword formula needs to first `@Explode`, and then `@Unique` the resulting `@DbColumn` list, as indicated in the first step.

Here is an example. Suppose we have documents which have already been categorized on these values:

Apples

Bananas, Eclairs

Bananas

Cookies

Apples, Bananas, Cookies

Cookies, Donuts

If you open this view on a Domino 7 server, you will correctly see:

Apples

Bananas

Cookies

Donuts

Eclairs

But on a Domino 6 server, you might see:

Apples

Apples,Bananas,Cookies

Bananas

Cookies

Eclairs

Here is the screenshot of what you might see on a Domino 6 server in a view that does not use **Generate unique keys in index:**

Categories
Apples
Apples,Bananas,Cookies
Bananas
Bananas,Eclairs
Cookies
Cookies,Donuts

The following screenshot shows you a view in Domino 6 server that uses **Generate unique keys in index**:

Categories
Apples
Apples,Bananas,Cookies
Bananas
Cookies
Eclairs

This is because by the time the view gets around to indexing the document with **Cookies** and **Donuts**, it has already indexed the document with **Cookies**. Since it sees **Cookies**, it dumps the new document, unfortunately losing **Donuts** in the process.

Note that in this case, the second view has correctly discarded the document with **Bananas**, since it already displays that value with the document that has **Bananas** and **Eclairs**. If you find this confusing, just open our sample Domino database on a Notes 7 client and a Notes 6 client (or Domino 6 server) and test it yourself.

In conclusion, if you might be using a Domino 6 server, then take the safe route and use the very slightly more cumbersome formula.

InViewEditing

InViewEditing is a brilliant (and often underutilized) feature in Notes. It allows you to set up a view to be editable in a way that's similar to a spreadsheet, with users tabbing between cells and editing right at the view level, without needing to open a document.

The advantages of InViewEditing are simplicity and performance. The downside is that you cannot rely on the built-in editing of a document that forms give you. With forms, when a user types into a field and saves the document, that value is stored (saved) into that field. When you use InViewEditing, all of this needs to be coded by the developer. In addition, your form events such as `PostOpen` and `QuerySave` are not triggered, so any data validation or synchronization, security checks, workflow, and so on will need to be coded explicitly, or else skipped entirely.

Therefore, before you use InViewEditing, you should carefully review your application and your data, and identify cases where being able to edit a handful of fields is useful and where the data to be edited is sufficiently straightforward to allow reasonably easy coding.

In this section, we first describe the "big picture" about using InViewEditing, and then get into some details. In our sample Domino database, the view InViewEditing demonstrates an example of InViewEditing in action. The code itself is in the View Design under InViewEdit (and also under Globals).

Overview: What does a User See and Do with InViewEditing?

When opening an InViewEditing-enabled view, you will not see anything out of the ordinary. But if you click on a document or press the *F2* key, you will enter Edit mode for the cell you are highlighting.

SalesRep	Categories	Comment
Raphael Savir	Bananas	
Fred Merkle	Apples	
Jane Merkle	Apples,Bananas,Cookies	first set of comments
Fred Merkle	Cookies	second set of comments
Betty J. Merkle	Cookies,Donuts	
Raphael Savir	Bananas,Eclairs	

You can now type anything you want and press the *Enter* or *Tab* key to save your changes. The *Enter* key will save the change and return you to your regular View mode. The *Tab* key will move you to the next cell on the same row. Once the last cell has been edited, the *Tab* key will act the same as *Enter*.

Note that there is no built-in input translation or input validation, the way there is for field formulas. Nor are there multiple data types, rich text buttons, or any of the other rich features users associate with editing in a form. So why bother? Because even if your form has 300 fields, and pages and pages of form events and validation formulas, your users may frequently need to make a very simple edit (for example, change the name of the person to whom a document is assigned). It would therefore be very useful to provide a fast and easy interface for them. That's exactly what InViewEditing can do.

So in short, you can use this view just as you would use any other view, but by clicking into a cell, you can enter a "streamlined" Edit mode.

Setting Up a View and Columns for InViewEditing

For you to set up a view for InViewEditing, you need to do two things. The first is to enable editing for each column that you want to be editable. On the first tab of Column Properties there is a setting called **Editable column**. Enable this setting, and immediately any user can click into a cell in that column and begin typing.

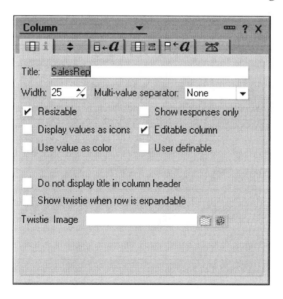

However, none of what users type will be saved to the back-end document unless you take the second step: writing code into the `InViewEdit` event of the view.

In addition to the InViewEditing example in our sample Domino database, the Domino Designer online help also has a working example of InViewEditing, which you can copy and paste to get started.

Points to Consider when Using InViewEdit

A few points to keep in mind as you write your code:

- Your code will need to determine which cell the user is in when he or she types, and then push that data into the back-end document in the appropriate field(s).

- The `InViewEdit` event will be called every time the user enters a cell, leaves a cell, or saves by pressing *Enter* (or, if on the last cell, pressing *Tab*). This means that your code should be very streamlined for performance.

- There is no built-in user interface for drop-down lists, which is a great way to ensure data integrity. In our example, we show how to implement a drop-down list, using a small amount of code.

- The user interface for input validation is somewhat crude. In our example, we show how to handle validation as cleanly as possible.

The Sample InViewEdit Code

The InViewEdit view in the sample database contains an example of the InViewEdit feature in action. In Global Declarations and Initialize events, we have written as much code as possible. This allows us to only have this portion of code executed one time, when the user opens the view, instead of every time they *Tab* into and out of a cell.

In the `InViewEdit` event, we start by ensuring that the user is in fact highlighting a document, and not a category. We do this using the following bit of code:

```
caret = Source.CaretNoteID
If caret = "0" Then Exit Sub
Set doc = db.GetDocumentByID ( caret )
```

This also gives us a handle to the back-end document, which we'll need when it's time to push information from the user's keyboard into the document.

We then determine what the user is doing. There are four possibilities:

- Query is the equivalent of going into Edit mode in a cell.
- Validate happens when you exit a cell.
- Save happens when the user presses *Enter* (or presses *Tab* when positioned at the last editable cell in the row).
- Create New Document is an option to allow you to create documents from the view without interacting with a form at all. Because this is only peripherally related to the basic editing functionality, we will skip this.

In Global Declarations, you can see the constants we use (straight from Domino Designer online help) to determine the user's actions.

The `InViewEdit` event gives us certain handles, including `Colprogname` and `Columnvalue`. `Colprogname (0)` is the programmable name of the column the user is working in. `Columnvalue (0)` is the data that is currently in that cell.

One of the time-saving techniques we use in our sample is to make sure that every editable column has a programmable name that is identical to the field name it corresponds to. So, for example, **SalesRep**, **Categories**, and **Comment** are the three columns in our view. The fact that the column heading shows these labels is irrelevant. What is relevant is that the first text box on the last tab of the column properties has these values.

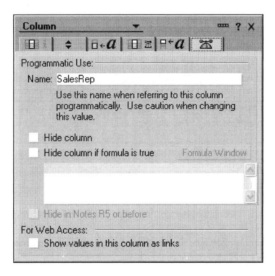

In our example code, we check to see whether the user is in the **SalesRep** or **Categories** columns, and if so, we display a dialog box that allows the user to select values from a list, with the current value included and highlighted in that list. The following shows the pop up for the **SalesRep** category:

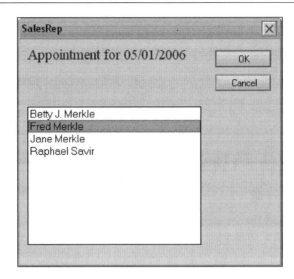

If the user is in the **Comment** column, then we allow the user to edit normally, without further intervention.

After the user has selected value(s) in the dialog box, we capture those values and then push them into the cell, using a subroutine called PushKeys. This reads the values and performs the keystrokes for each character. If we were only concerned about the back-end document, we could push the data directly there without worrying about the on-screen interface. However, it will look very strange to users if they choose values and don't see those new values reflected on-screen when they move onto the next cell.

Because we are using a very modular approach to how we push the data into the back-end document, you could add new editable columns to this view without having to write a single line of code. Try it! Add a column with the following characteristics:

1. **Column Heading** (label) can be anything you want. Make this an editable column by enabling the **Editable column** checkbox in the first tab of Column properties.

2. **Column formula** should be a field reference, to the field called Comment2.

3. **Column Programmable Name** (last tab of column properties) should also be Comment2.

And that's it. Just save the view and start using InViewEditing as a user. You'll see that whatever you type into your new column is saved into the back-end document in the Comment2 field.

Tips

From working with InViewEditing for some time, we have come up with some tips you might find helpful:

- Use editable columns only for direct field references, not for concatenations of multiple fields. For example, a formula like the following one would just cause a lot of trouble in your InViewEdit code:

  ```
  Subject + " (" + @Name([Abbreviate]; Author) + " - " +
                @Text(@Date(LastEditDate)) + ")"
  ```

- Always make the programmatic name of the column the same as the field you are referencing.

- Note that whatever a user types in will be regarded as text, even if it looks like a date or a name, so you'll have to code the data type translation

- Drop-down lists are not supported, so you'll have to code them yourself. The InViewEdit view in our application has two of these, which can be copied and pasted as a template. They use dialog boxes for superior user interface and input validation.

- Input validation is not handled well natively. There is a Validation mode, but if you pop up a box telling the user that they need to fix something (for instance, a blank entry) then it'll get yet another pop-up box with a generic error message when the Save mode is triggered. This means that if you can handle input validation through dialog boxes, you'll give your users a better experience.

- Un-remark some of the debugging lines of code that we've put into the InViewEdit code, and run through a few edits as a user. It's a very enlightening experience in terms of seeing when the InViewEdit event is called, how validation is handled, and so on.

Summary

In this chapter, we've reviewed several examples of new programming features offered in Lotus Notes/Domino 7. These included the **Save & Close** action bar button, preventing editing of fields and documents dynamically, fast DBLookups, and InViewEditing. The code examples we discussed in this chapter can be found in our sample Domino database, which you can download at http://www.packtpub.com/support. By using these and the other examples contained in our sample database, you can get a head start on taking advantage of these features in your own Notes/Domino applications.

11

Troubleshooting Applications

In this chapter, we'll examine several tips and techniques for identifying and correcting problems in your Notes/Domino 7 applications. This includes troubleshooting issues that affect performance. (For more on optimizing performance in your Notes/Domino applications, see Chapter 9.)

The major topics that we'll cover in this chapter are:

- Testing your application (in other words, uncovering problems before your users do it for you).
- Asking the right questions when users do discover problems.
- Using logging to help troubleshoot your problems.

We'll also examine two important new Notes/Domino 7 features that can be critical for troubleshooting applications:

- Domino Domain Monitoring (DDM)
- Agent Profiler

Testing your Application

Testing an application before you roll it out to your users may sound like an obvious thing to do. However, during the life cycle of a project, testing is often not allocated adequate time or money.

Proper testing should include the following:

- *A meaningful amount of developer testing and bug fixing*: This allows you to catch most errors, which saves time and frustration for your user community.

- *User representative testing*: A user representative, who is knowledgeable about the application and how users use it, can often provide more robust testing than the developer. This also provides early feedback on features.

- *Pilot testing*: In this phase, the product is assumed to be complete, and a pilot group uses it in production mode. This allows for limited stress testing as well as more thorough testing of the feature set.

In addition to feature testing, you should test the performance of the application. This is the most frequently skipped type of testing, because some consider it too complex and difficult. In fact, it can be difficult to test user load, but in general, it's not difficult to test data load. So, as part of any significant project, it is a good practice to programmatically create the projected number of documents that will exist within the application, one or two years after it has been fully deployed, and have a scheduled agent trigger the appropriate number of edits-per-hour during the early phases of feature testing.

Although this will not give a perfect picture of performance, it will certainly help ascertain whether and why the time to create a new document is unacceptable (for example, because the @Db formulas are taking too long, or because the scheduled agent that runs every 15 minutes takes too long due to slow document searches).

Asking the Right Questions

Suppose that you've rolled out your application and people are using it. Then the support desk starts getting calls about a certain problem. Maybe your boss is getting an earful at meetings about sluggish performance or is hearing gripes about error messages whenever users try to click a button to perform some action.

In this section, we will discuss a methodology to help you troubleshoot a problem when you don't necessarily have all the information at your disposal. We will include some specific questions that can be asked verbatim for virtually any application.

The first key to success in troubleshooting an application problem is to narrow down where and when it happens. Let's take these two very different problems suggested above (slow performance and error messages), and pose questions that might help unravel them:

- *Does the problem occur when you take a specific action? If so, what is that action?* Your users might say, "It's slow whenever I open the application", or "I get an error when I click this particular button in this particular form".

- *Does the problem occur for everyone who does this, or just for certain people? If just certain people, what do they have in common?*

This is a great way to get your users to help you help them. Let them be a part of the solution, not just "messengers of doom". For example, you might ask questions such as, "Is it slow only for people in your building or your floor? Is it slow only for people accessing the application remotely? Is it slow only for people who have your particular access (for example, **SalesRep**)?"

- *Does this problem occur all the time, at random times, or only at certain times?* It's helpful to check whether or not the time of day or the day of week/month is relevant. So typical questions might be similar to the following: "Do you get this error every time you click the button or just sometimes? If just sometimes, does it give you the error during the middle of the day, but not if you click it at 7 AM when you first arrive? Do you only get the error on Mondays or some other day of the week? Do you only see the error if the document is in a certain status or has certain data in it? If it just happens for a particular document, please send me a link to that document so that I can inspect it carefully to see if there is invalid or unexpected data."

Logging

Ideally, your questions have narrowed down the type of problem it could be. So at this point, the more technical troubleshooting can start. You will likely need to gather concrete information to confirm or refine what you're hearing from the users. For example, you could put a bit of debugging code into the button that they're clicking so that it gives more informative errors, or sends you an email (or creates a log document) whenever it's clicked or whenever an error occurs. Collecting the following pieces of information might be enough to diagnose the problem very quickly:

- Time/date
- User name
- Document UNID (if the button is pushed in a document)
- Error
- Status or any other likely field that might affect your code

By looking for common denominators (such as the status of the documents in question, or access or roles of the users), you will likely be able to further narrow down the possibilities of why the problem is happening. This doesn't solve your problem of course, but it helps in advancing you a long way towards that goal.

A trickier problem to troubleshoot might be one we mentioned earlier: slow performance. Typically, after you've determined that there is some kind of performance delay, it's a good idea to first collect some server logging data. Set the following `Notes.ini` variables in the Server Configuration document in your Domino Directory, on the `Notes.ini` tab:

```
Log_Update=1
Log_AgentManager=1
```

These variables instruct the server to write output to the `log.nsf` database in the Miscellaneous Events view. Note that they may already be set in your environment. If not, they're fairly unobtrusive, and shouldn't trouble your administration group. Set them for a 24-hour period during a normal business week, and then examine the results to see if anything pops out as being suspicious.

For view indexing, you should look for lines like these in the Miscellaneous Events (`Log_Update=1`):

```
07/01/2006 09:29:57 AM   Updating views in apps\SalesPipeline.nsf
07/01/2006 09:30:17 AM   Finished updating views in
                                        apps\SalesPipeline.nsf
07/01/2006 09:30:17 AM   Updating views in apps\Tracking.nsf
07/01/2006 09:30:17 AM   Finished updating views in apps\Tracking.nsf
07/01/2006 09:30:17 AM   Updating views in apps\ZooSchedule.nsf
07/01/2006 09:30:18 AM   Finished updating views in
                                        apps\ZooSchedule.nsf
```

And lines like these for Agent execution (`Log_AgentManager=1`):

```
06/30/2006 09:43:49 PM   AMgr: Start executing agent 'UpdateTickets'
                         in 'apps\SalesPipeline.nsf ' by Executive '1'
06/30/2006 09:43:52 PM   AMgr: Start executing agent 'ZooUpdate' in
                              'apps\ZooSchedule.nsf ' by Executive '2'
06/30/2006 09:44:44 PM   AMgr: Start executing agent 'DirSynch' in
                              'apps\Tracking.nsf ' by Executive '1'
```

Let's examine these lines to see whether or not there is anything we can glean from them. Starting with the `Log_Update=1` setting, we see that it gives us the start and stop times for every database that gets indexed. We also see that the database file paths appear alphabetically. This means that, if we search for the text string `updating views` and pull out all these lines covering (for instance) an hour during a busy part of the day, and copy/paste these lines into a text editor so that they're all together, then we should see complete database indexing from A to Z on your server repeating every so often.

In the `log.nsf` database, there may be many thousands of lines that have nothing to do with your investigation, so culling the important lines is imperative for you to be able to make any sense of what's going on in your environment.

You will likely see dozens or even hundreds of databases referenced. If you have hundreds of active databases on your server, then culling all these lines might be impractical, even programmatically. Instead, you might focus on the largest group of databases. You will notice that the same databases are referenced every so often. This is the Update Cycle, or view indexing cycle. It's important to get a sense of how long this cycle takes, so make sure you don't miss any references to your group of databases.

Imagine that `SalesPipeline.nsf` and `Tracking.nsf` were the two databases that you wanted to focus on. You might cull the lines out of the log that have `updating views` and which reference these two databases, and come up with something like the following:

```
07/01/2006 09:29:57 AM  Updating views in apps\SalesPipeline.nsf
07/01/2006 09:30:17 AM  Finished updating views in
                                        apps\SalesPipeline.nsf
07/01/2006 09:30:17 AM  Updating views in apps\Tracking.nsf
07/01/2006 09:30:20 AM  Finished updating views in apps\Tracking.nsf

07/01/2006 10:15:55 AM  Updating views in apps\SalesPipeline.nsf
07/01/2006 10:16:33 AM  Finished updating views in
                                        apps\SalesPipeline.nsf
07/01/2006 10:16:33 AM  Updating views in apps\Tracking.nsf
07/01/2006 10:16:43 AM  Finished updating views in apps\Tracking.nsf

07/01/2006 11:22:31 AM  Updating views in apps\SalesPipeline.nsf
07/01/2006 11:23:33 AM  Finished updating views in
                                        apps\SalesPipeline.nsf
07/01/2006 11:23:33 AM  Updating views in apps\Tracking.nsf
07/01/2006 11:23:44 AM  Finished updating views in apps\Tracking.nsf
```

This gives us some very important information: the Update task (view indexing) is taking approximately an hour to cycle through the databases on the server; that's too long. The Update task is supposed to run every 15 minutes, and ideally should only run for a few minutes each time it executes. If the cycle is an hour, then that means update is running full tilt for that hour, and as soon as it stops, it realizes that it's overdue and kicks off again.

It's possible that if you examine each line in the log, you'll find that certain databases are taking the bulk of the time, in which case it might be worth examining the design of those databases. But it might be that every database seems to take a long time, which might be more indicative of a general server slowdown.

In any case, we haven't solved the problem; but at least we know that the problem is probably server-wide. More complex applications, and newer applications, tend to reflect server-performance problems more readily, but that doesn't necessarily mean they carry more responsibility for the problem. In a sense, they are the "canary in the coal mine".

If you suspect the problem is confined to one database (or a few), then you can increase the logging detail by setting Log_Update=2. This will give you the start time for every view in every database that the Update task indexes. If you see particular views taking a long time, then you can examine the design of those views.

If no database(s) stand out, then you might want to see if the constant indexing occurs around the clock or just during business hours. If it's around the clock, then this might point to some large quantities of data that are changing in your databases. For example, you may be programmatically synchronizing many gigabytes of data throughout the day, not realizing the cost this brings in terms of indexing.

If slow indexing only occurs during business hours, then perhaps the user/data load has not been planned out well for this server. As the community of users ramps up in the morning, the server starts falling behind and never catches up until evening. There are server statistics that can help you determine whether or not this is the case. (These server statistics go beyond the scope of this book, but you can begin your investigation by searching on the various Notes/Domino forums for "server AND performance AND statistics".)

As may be obvious at this point, troubleshooting can be quite time-consuming. The key is to make sure that you think through each step so that it either eliminates something important, or gives you a forward path. Otherwise, you can find yourself still gathering information weeks and months later, with users and management feeling very frustrated.

Before moving on from this section, let's take a quick look at agent logging. Agent Manager can run multiple agents in different databases, as determined by settings in your server document. Typically, production servers only allow two or three concurrent agents to run during business hours, and these are marked in the log as Executive '1', Executive '2', and so on.

If your server is often busy with agent execution, then you can track Executive '1' and see how many different agents it runs, and for how long. If there are big gaps between when one agent starts and when the next one does (for Executive '1'), this might raise suspicion that the first agent took that whole time to execute. To verify this, turn up the logging by setting the Notes.ini variable debug_amgr=*. (This will output a fair amount of information into your log, so it's best not to leave it on for too long, but normally one day is not a problem.) Doing this will give you a very important piece of information: the number of "ticks" it took for the agent to run. One second equals 100 ticks, so if the agent takes 246,379 ticks, this equals 2,463 seconds (about 41 minutes).

As a general rule, you want scheduled agents to run in seconds, not minutes; so any agent that is taking this long will require some examination. In the next section, we will talk about some other ways you can identify problematic agents.

Domino Domain Monitoring (DDM)

Every once in a while, a killer feature is introduced—a feature so good, so important, so helpful, that after using it, we just shake our heads and wonder how we ever managed without it for so long. **Domino Domain Monitor (DDM)** is just such a feature.

DDM is too large to be completely covered in this one section, so we will confine our overview to what it can do in terms of troubleshooting applications. For a more thorough explanation of DDM and all its features, see the book, *Upgrading to Lotus Notes and Domino 7* (`www.packtpub.com/upgrading_lotus/book`).

In the `events4.nsf` database, you will find a new group of documents you can create for tracking agent or application performance. On Domino 7 servers, a new database is created automatically with the filename `ddm.nsf`. This stores the DDM output you will examine.

For application troubleshooting, some of the most helpful areas to track using DDM are the following:

- *Full-text index needs to be built*. If you have agents that are creating a full-text index on the fly because the database has no full-text index built, DDM can track that potential problem for you. Especially useful is the fact that DDM compiles the frequency per database, so (for instance) you can see if it happens once per month or once per hour. Creating full-text indexes on the fly can result in a significant demand on server resources, so having this notification is very useful. We discuss an example of this later in this section.

- *Agent security warnings*. You can manually examine the log to try to find errors about agents not being able to execute due to insufficient access. However, DDM will do this for you, making it much easier to find (and therefore fix) such problems.

- *Resource utilization*. You can track memory, CPU, and time utilization of your agents as run by Agent Manager or by the HTTP task. This means that at any time you can open the `ddm.nsf` database and spot the worst offenders in these categories, over your entire server/domain. We will discuss an example of CPU usage later in this section.

The following illustration shows the new set of DDM views in the `events4.nsf` (Monitoring configuration) database:

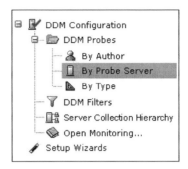

The following screenshot displays the **By Probe Server** view after we've made a few document edits:

7	2	⊟Application Code			
1	0	⊟Agents Behind Schedule			
		⊘ Default Application Code/Agents Behind Schedule Probe	Lotus Notes Template Development	07/21/2005 11:02:30 AM	Lotus Notes Template Development
2	1	⊟Agents Evaluated by CPU Usage			
		⊗ Default Application Code/Agents Evaluated By CPU Usage (Agent Manager)	Raphael Savir	07/02/2006 12:56:29 PM	Lotus Notes Template Development
		⊘ Default Application Code/Agents Evaluated By CPU Usage (HTTP)	Lotus Notes Template Development	07/21/2005 11:02:30 AM	Lotus Notes Template Development
2	1	⊟Agents Evaluated by Memory Usage			
		⊗ Default Application Code/Agents Evaluated By Memory Usage (Agent Manager)	Raphael Savir	07/02/2006 12:57:18 PM	Lotus Notes Template Development
		⊘ Default Application Code/Agents Evaluated By Memory Usage (HTTP)	Lotus Notes Template Development	07/21/2005 11:02:30 AM	Lotus Notes Template Development
2	0	⊟Long Running Agents			
		⊘ Default Application Code/Long Running Agents (Agent Manager)	Lotus Notes Template Development	07/21/2005 11:02:30 AM	Lotus Notes Template Development
		⊘ Default Application Code/Long Running Agents (HTTP)	Lotus Notes Template Development	07/21/2005 11:02:30 AM	Lotus Notes Template Development
5	1	⊟**Database**			
1	0	⊟Database Compact			
		⊘ Default Database/Compact Probe	Lotus Notes Template Development	07/21/2005 11:02:30 AM	Lotus Notes Template Development
1	0	⊟Database Design			
		⊘ Default Database/Design Probe	Lotus Notes Template Development	07/21/2005 11:02:30 AM	Lotus Notes Template Development
2	1	⊟Database Error Monitoring			
		⊗ Db Errors (including ft index)	Raphael Savir	07/02/2006 01:01:32 PM	Raphael Savir
		⊘ Default Database/Error Monitoring Probe	Lotus Notes Template Development	07/21/2005 11:02:30 AM	Lotus Notes Template Development

Notice that there are many probes included out-of-the-box (identified by the property "author = Lotus Notes Template Development") but set to disabled. In this view, there are three that have been enabled (ones with checkmarks) and were created by one of the authors of this book.

If you edit the probe document highlighted above, **Default Application Code/ Agents Evaluated By CPU Usage (Agent Manager)**, the document consists of three sections.

The first section is where you choose the type of probe (in this case **Application Code**) and the subtype (in this case **Agents Evaluated By CPU Usage**).

The second section allows you to choose the servers to run against, and whether you want this probe to run against agents/code executed by Agent Manager or by the HTTP task (as shown in the following screenshot).

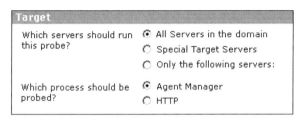

This is an important distinction. For one thing, they are different tasks, and therefore one can hit a limit while the other still has room to "breathe". But perhaps more significantly, if you choose a subtype of **Agents Evaluated By Memory Usage**, then the algorithms used to evaluate whether or not an agent is using too much memory are very different. Agents run by the HTTP task will be judged much more harshly than those run by the Agent Manager task. This is because with the HTTP task, it is possible to run the same agent with up to hundreds of thousands of concurrent executions. But with Agent Manager, you are effectively limited to ten concurrent instances, and none within the same database.

The third section allows you to set your threshold for when DDM should report the activity:

Event generation status:	Evaluation by CPU seconds used:	Generate an event of severity:
☐ Enabled	60 seconds	Fatal
☑ Enabled	60 seconds	Failure
☑ Enabled	6 seconds	Warning (High)
☐ Enabled	180 seconds	Warning (Low)

You can select up to four levels of warning: **Fatal**, **Failure**, **Warning (High)**, and **Warning (Low)**. Note that you do not have the ability to change the severity labels (which appear as icons in the view). Unless you change the database design of ddm.nsf, the icons displayed in the view and documents are non-configurable.

Experiment with these settings until you find the approach that is most useful for your corporation. Typically, customers start by overwhelming themselves with information, and then fine-tuning the probes so that much less information is reported. In this example, only two statuses are enabled: one for six seconds, with a label of **Warning (High)**, and one for 60 seconds, with a label of **Failure**.

Here is a screenshot of the DDM database:

Notice that there are two Application Code results, one with a status of **Failure** (because that agent ran for more than 60 seconds), and one with a status of **Warning (High)** (because that agent ran for more than six seconds but less than 60 seconds). These are the parameters set in the Probe document shown previously, which can easily be changed by editing that Probe document. If you want these labels to be different, you must enable different rows in the Probe document.

If you open one of these documents, there are three sections. The top section gives header information about this event, such as the server name, the database and agent name, and so on. The second section includes the following table, with a tab for the most recent infraction and a tab for previous infractions. This allows you to see how often the problem is occurring, and with what severity.

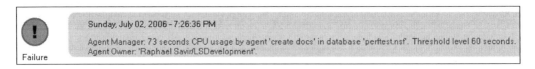

The third section provides some possible solutions, and (if applicable) automation. For example, in our example, you might want to "profile" your agent. (We will profile one of our agents in the final section of this chapter.)

DDM can capture full-text operations against a database that is not full-text indexed. It tracks the number of times this happens, so you can decide whether to full-text index the database, change the agent, or neither.

For a more complete list of the errors and problems that DDM can help resolve, check the Domino 7 online help or the product documentation (www.lotus.com).

Agent Profiler

If any of the troubleshooting tips or techniques we've discussed in this chapter causes you to look at an agent and think, "I wonder what makes this agent so slow", then the Agent Profiler should be the next tool to consider. **Agent Profiler** is another new feature introduced in Notes/Domino 7. It gives you a breakdown of many methods/properties in your LotusScript agent, telling you how often each one was executed and how long they took to execute.

In Notes/Domino 7, the second (security) tab of Agent properties now includes a checkbox labeled **Profile this agent**. You can select this option if you want an agent to be profiled.

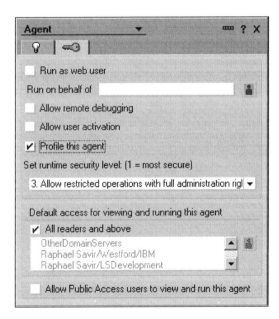

The next time the agent runs, a profile document in the database is created and filled with the information from that execution. This document is then updated every time the agent runs. You can view these results from the Agent View by highlighting your agent and selecting **Agent | View Profile Results**.

The following is a profile for an agent that performed slow mail searches:

Mail Agent - db.search Profile

07/03/2006 09:41:03 AM EDT
Elapsed time: 56461 msec
Methods profiled: 12
Total measured time: 50942 msec

Class	Method	Operation	Calls	Time
Database	Search		6	43392
DocumentCollection	GetNextDocument		15535	6519
Database	Open		30	731
Document	Size	Get	15535	210
DocumentCollection	GetFirstDocument		6	80
DbDirectory	GetNextDatabase		30	10
Database	Title	Get	30	0
Database	FilePath	Get	30	0
Database	Size	Get	30	0
Session	CurrentDatabase	Get	1	0
Session	GetDbDirectory		1	0
DbDirectory	GetFirstDatabase		1	0

Although this doesn't completely measure (and certainly does not completely troubleshoot) your agents, it is an important step forward in troubleshooting code. Imagine the alternative: dozens of print statements, and then hours of collating results!

Summary

In closing, we hope that this chapter has opened your eyes to new possibilities in troubleshooting, both in terms of techniques and new Notes/Domino 7 features. Every environment has applications that users wish ran faster, but with a bit of care, you can troubleshoot your performance problems and find resolutions.

After you have your servers running Notes/Domino 7, you can use DDM and Agent Profiler (both exceptionally easy to use) to help nail down poorly performing code in your applications. These tools really open a window on what had previously been a room full of mysterious behavior. Full-text indexing on the fly, code that uses too much memory, and long running agents are all quickly identified by DDM. Try it!

A
Vendor Tools

In this appendix, we review several vendor tools that you can use to help upgrade your applications to Lotus Notes/Domino 7. These include:

- Angkor by Atlantic Decisions
- PistolStar Password Power 8 Plug-ins by PistolStar, Inc
- CMT Inspector from Binary Tree
- FT Search Manager from IONET

Angkor

Angkor™ is a tool developed by Atlantic Decisions, Inc., to provide a means to analyzing an entire Lotus Domino/Notes enterprise infrastructure in a short period of time. It was built to help Notes managers get a handle on the mass of activity and data that makes up the typical thriving Notes installation. Some of the typical *noncritical* issues facing today's managers are:

- The need to cut costs, without affecting essential business services.
- Upgrading: database compatibility testing.
- Determining which Notes applications should be migrated.
- Implementing (or tightening) mail quotas: what are the true costs / opportunities?

In most installations, up to *a third* of all databases could be eliminated without significant impact on the business. It is not very difficult, given the appropriate data and knowing that it is current and accurate. If you can eliminate all the databases that are not being used effectively, costs will go down. An upgrade would also be easy, but someone has to figure out how much it will cost to test all of the applications, and budget for the development time to fix them. It is better to know these details before the project starts.

How Angkor Works

Angkor searches out every server in the domain, then every database on those servers. A complete inventory is provided with data such as size, number of documents, and template. The data is *rolled up* to the server and application levels for additional visibility. Views that consolidate replicas are included. Angkor lets you see a complete picture of the Notes infrastructure, allowing you to compare the various parts on a one-to-one basis. The following is an example of an Angkor inventory:

Notes/Domino Inventory === Infrastructure Mapping

Domain verification report	
Server discovery	
Connection report	
Database discovery	
Database access report	

Mail Inventory === Including for each mail file:

Template version	Mail impact by user
Size	Consolidates size, usage, and # of docs to ID top users
Document count	Mail-enabled applications - cost and impact
Location	Server / Path / Filename

Database Inventory === Including for each database:

Template version	Db sorted by usage, individually, and "rolled up"
Size	Application usage
Document count	Server usage
Location	Template Diversity Report

Replica Report

Identified replica copies	Including locations across all servers
Non-replica copies	Copies of existing databases that do not replicate. Including locations across all servers.

Server Report

Server level "rollups"	Of all database and mail data for each server.

Categorization Reports

All databases by general type	- Mail	- 3rd party applications

All databases by general type	- Mail	- 3rd party applications
	- Applications	- Lotus applications
Sorted by	- Server	- Database
	- Domain	
Graphical depictions	Of server and database statistics.	
	Docs vs db's vs MB	

Usage

Notes user listings for all databases

Databases report with primary users for each database ("owners")

In subsequent phases, Angkor extracts the complete usage history and design specifications, in detail, for each database. Reports integrate the data to show which servers, applications, and databases are the most heavily used — a critical data point for any decision (see below).

Consolidation Reports

Duplicate file instances report

Lotus Help and Documentation databases report

Standard Lotus databases created at installation — rarely used.

Mail file and server consolidation options

Databases by replica ID, all multiples included

Organizational Cost Figures

Departmental or other organizational rollups of mail figures

Departmental or other organizational rollups of application figures

Security Report

Discrepancies across replicas, use of special features (encryption, controlled sections, etc.), default access, manager).

Custom Reporting

AD can build additional Angkor usage/analysis reports according to customer specific requirements.

Application Complexity Report

This report provides an in-depth analysis of every element of all Domino applications, and catalogues them within the application for easy review.

Selected databases	Specific applications as identified
Application rollups (replicas)	Consolidated reports for replicated applications
Code elements	Lotuscripts, etc. within the application
Design elements	Notes structure, views, forms, agents, and ACL
Weighting	Relative "weights" used to calculate an accurate, level scale to measure complexity
Categories include	- Mail - Databases
	- Applications - Domains
	- Organization - Cost vs. Usage
	- Cost vs. Age

Best Practices/Code Efficiency

Code	Identifies code elements for opportunities to improve efficiency, points to potential problem areas
Resource usage	Identifies known problem areas within Notes design
Custom analysis	Rules-based engine allows flexibility

R7 Migration

R7 compatibility	Identifies potential R6 problems within applications
Code-walker	Direct linking to specific problem code segments

Custom Reporting

The complexity of the individual databases in terms of both design and code is provided, so the true cost of the infrastructure can be accounted for in detail. All of this is built into a set of Notes databases that provide the precise information needed. These databases are left with you, with design elements exposed, for further analysis and review.

A rules-based analysis engine provides custom searches for design elements with potential upgrade issues. Or it can search out elements that are adaptable or problematic for other technologies. Angkor allows for thousands of man-hours of detail analysis on your Notes applications and mail files. It provides useful data to help you make quality decisions now, and not months from now. Most businesses, even if they have the staff to undertake these analyses, don't have the kind of time it takes to wait for a manual effort to be completed.

Results

Angkor compresses a major Notes analysis effort into a matter of days or weeks, giving both an overview and the detail necessary for plans to be made, justifications documented, and actions taken. Information such as Angkor provides should be the first step in any major Notes/Domino project, something that has never been available before.

The detail analysis of code and design elements allows for a wide range of custom reports and analysis, depending upon customer requirements. Certain Notes elements may be sought out by the customer for conversion or support issues. It also allows for differing applications to be compared to one another with a standardized measure of their complexity, providing a valuable tool for users to compare their application base against standards such as the Notes mail file.

PistolStar Password Power 8 Plug-Ins

PistolStar Inc. is a password management software solutions provider specializing in IBM software platforms, with a core focus on the Lotus software suite. Many of PistolStar's senior-level developers are from Iris and Lotus, bringing in-depth knowledge and first hand experience to Password Power 8 plug-ins.

PistolStar's Password Power 8 plug-ins expand the authentication and password management capabilities of Lotus Domino 7. The Domino plug-in offers HTTP SSO to Domino and seamless redirection of HTTP authentication to LDAP-compliant directories (for example, Microsoft Active Directory, Novell eDirectory), while the **Web Set Password** plug-in (**WSP**) offers great control over the management of the Domino Internet password if it is vital to the current authentication processes. This section outlines the functionality available with each of PistolStar's Password Power 8 plug-ins as they pertain to Lotus Domino7.

To achieve PistolStar's definition of **Single Sign-On (SSO)**, we start at the desktop with the Windows session. We leverage Microsoft Active Directory and Novell eDirectory—both significant technologies in Windows-centric computer environments—by enabling use of either of their passwords at the initial computer login to access all Domino server applications in multiple domains and the Notes client. With this capability, the number of times an end-user must supply logon information during a Windows session is reduced to a single instance.

Password Power 8 Domino Plug-In

The Domino plug-in provides end-users with SSO access to all applications on Domino servers in multiple DNS domains (for example, `sametime.pistolstar.com` and `sametime.pistolstar.us`), creating convenience and saving login time. To enable SSO to Domino HTTP servers, a web browser toolbar creates client-side cookies with encrypted credentials for each of the Domino servers listed in the Password Power configuration file. Accessing a Domino server through a web browser automatically sends the corresponding cookie with the request. These same cookies can also be used to grant SSO to:

- IBM Lotus QuickPlace
- IBM Lotus Sametime
- IBM WebSphere
- IBM WebSphere Portal
- SAP Netweaver

These in-memory session cookies have a configurable expiration interval that defaults to 12 hours. When the end-user closes the browser, logs out, or shuts down Windows, the cookies are automatically destroyed.

The Domino plug-in also allows the end-user to log in to Domino HTTP with their network login or LDAP-compliant directory credentials. This functionality solves many of the username mapping issues associated with Directory Assistance without requiring changes to the LDAP server accounts, Domino Directory, Domino groups, or ACLs. Redirecting web-authentication requests from the Domino Directory to a different LDAP directory also eliminates the need to maintain or synchronize the Domino Internet password, as its presence and upkeep are no longer required. This functionality extends to affect all Domino HTTP authentication including QuickPlace and Sametime.

Password Power 8 Web Set Password Plug-In

This plug-in synchronizes multiple passwords via a web browser. This allows end-users to synchronize Windows, HTTP, LDAP passwords, and Notes ID File. This increases security because having only one password to commit to memory decreases the likelihood that end-users will write it down and become a target for internal intruders.

Security

The Password Power 8 Web Set Password plug-in (WSP) offers the following security features:

- *Force an SSL connection for logins*: WSP can ensure that end-users' credentials are submitted via SSL. If an end-user tries to log in through HTTP instead of HTTPS, WSP forces login with HTTPS by redirecting the end-user to a HTTPS connection.

- *Dictionary lookup functionality*: This allows administrators to enable a dictionary lookup to prevent users from setting pre-specified (unacceptable or easily guessed) passwords such as the company name. The lookup can be added in three ways: Notes database, JavaScript, or both Notes database and a list accessed through JavaScript.

- *Password quality*: With WSP, administrators can configure 12 fully customizable password "strength" rules:
  Minimum length
  Password cannot contain the username
  Password cannot be on a customized list of words
  Password cannot be similar to current password
  Password must contain a configurable number of numeric characters
  Password must contain a "special" character (from a customizable list)
  Password must contain a configurable number of lower characters
  Password must contain a configurable number of upper characters
  Password cannot be a previously used password
  Password cannot be any variant of the end-user's username
  Password cannot be a dictionary word (used for lists of 10,000+ words)
  Minimum "quality" as defined by @PasswordQuality formula

- *Password quality checks on both client and server sides*: With WSP, client-side checking does not access the server, and is done through JavaScript requiring less server load and network traffic. Server-side checking can use @PasswordQuality instead of JavaScript (requires a trip to the server) to determine if a new password is acceptable. This allows administrators to set minimum password quality (0-16) and any new password must, as a minimum, equal this quality.

- *Maintain HTTP password history*: Configurable history limits allow administrators to set how many times an end-user must choose a new password before they can reuse an old one, preventing the end-user from using the same password over and over again.

- *Disqualify username as password*: Administrators can prevent new passwords from containing variations of the end-user's username, a typical password choice that is easily guessed by network intruders.

- *Configurable "Expire on First Login"*: This ensures that end-users will not continue to use the password issued by the administrator when the end-user account was first set up.

- *Configurable password expiration intervals*: This allows administrators to set intervals between end-users' password resets (for example, every 15 or 30 days).

- *Password expiration grace period*: WSP lets administrators select a grace period or a time frame in which end-users must change their passwords.

- *Strikeout limit functionality*: WSP allows administrators to set how many login attempts can be made before the end-user strikes out, preventing dictionary attacks and identifying accounts that have been denied server access.

- *Disable Internet Explorer auto-complete*: Administrators can prevent Internet Explorer's auto-complete feature from offering a list of previously used entries. When enabled, this applies to all WSP fields, and only affects IS5.0 and higher. This feature prevents internal intruders from easily accessing the password from the drop-down menu of previously used passwords.

- *Prevent similar password use*: WSP's "Prevent Similar Passwords" JavaScript Rule checking disallows use of similar passwords during password resets.

- *Confirmation requirement for self-registration*. With WSP, an email is sent to the end-user with a link to a confirmation page for self-registration. On this page, end-users are prompted for their email address, which affects creation of the Person document in the Domino Directory.

Auditing Features

WSP also includes auditing features. These include:

- *Store last login date and time*: Administrators can track the date and time an end-user last logged in – data that is stored as a new field in the Person document. Administrators can also elect to record more detailed information to be sent to the WSP database, such as username, end-user's IP address, URL requested, and server name.

- *Enable strikeout logging functionality*: Strikeouts can be logged to a database so that administrators can see when failed attempts occurred.

- *Store "set password" date and time*: Administrators can track the date and time an end-user last set his or her HTTP password – data stored as a new field in the Person document.

- *Log passwords used*: With WSP, administrators can enable logging of 'Password Used' when a Strikeout, Strike, or Invalid Username event is logged to the mail-in database.

- *Log invalid usernames*: Administrators can enable logging of invalid usernames to the mail-in database. The information included in this report is: IP address of the computer that made the request

URL requested by the user
Username used
Password given
The WSP-specific function the user attempted to accomplish (log in, set
password, and so on)
The server on which the attempt occurred
The time the attempt occurred

- *Enable "set password" logging.* In WSP, administrators can enable logging of
  successful "Set Password" events to the mail-in database.

Help Desk

WSP also includes Help Desk productivity features. For example, WSP's Help Desk
Manager Utility allows Help Desk personnel to manage end-user passwords without
full access to WSP's configuration data. This database includes seven action buttons:

- **Unlock User**: unlocks end-user accounts that have been locked by WSP's
  strikeout function utility.

- **Email Random Password**: generates random value passwords and emails
  them to the end-user. This can also be used to automatically send multiple
  end-users' blank passwords.

- **Reset Password**: resets the HTTP password to a new value when an
  end-user does not have an HTTP password, has forgotten it, is unable to
  reset it themselves, and does not have a Notes client.

- **Expire Password**: forces end-users to change their HTTP password the next
  time they log in to Domino through a web browser. This is useful when
  password policies change.

- **Reset WSP Fields**: resets end-user accounts as if they had never accessed WSP.

- **Set Expiration Date**: provides a one-time override of WSP's expiration
  functionality. This is useful for exempting end-users from resetting
  a password.

- **Unlock Agent**: unlocks end-users automatically every x number of hours.

In addition, WSP offers the following features designed to assist Help Desk personnel:

- *Enable customized HTML*: With WSP, administrators can write customized
  messages to end-users to prompt them through the login process, reducing
  end-user confusion and subsequent Help Desk calls.

- *Email Random Password Functionality*: Administrators can generate random
  passwords that are automatically emailed to new end-users. This is both
  an administrative time-saver as well as a security feature because the
  administrator never sees the password. WSP enables customizable expiration
  options for the new password as well.

- *Support localization*: Administrators can configure all UI screens in any language without the use/knowledge of Domino Designer. Administrators can easily modify logon screens to ensure that customized messages and prompts are understood by the end-user. Localization reduces Help Desk calls by minimizing end-user confusion.

- *Enable customized disclaimer messages*: Administrators can create a disclaimer message that the end-user sees upon login. This feature can be used to display corporate network usage instructions for sensitive websites and resources (that are password protected).

- *Easily configurable user interface*: All WSP screens seen by the end-user are configurable without the knowledge/use of Domino Designer. Through a user-friendly interface, c\screens can be modified with logo insertion, font and color selection, and editing of HTML seen by the user.

- *WSP Unlock Utility*: WSP's strikeout functionality is an important part of securing the authentication process. When enabled, the end-user is no longer able to log in after a preset number of attempts. The WSP Unlock Utility allows Help Desk personnel who do not have editor-level access to the Domino directories to unlock end-users who have struck out.

You can now delegate unlocking of strikeouts to Help Desk personnel with less security clearance. This is especially beneficial to companies with employees in different time zones, when employing Help Desk personnel with a high-level of security clearance around the clock is costly. The end-user does not have to wait for support, and the company can maintain security by granting editor-level access to fewer personnel.

End-Users

WSP also offers end-user productivity features. For instance, WSP's challenge, question, and answer functionality allows the end-user to recover passwords without Help Desk assistance. This feature stems potential security breaches that occur when administrators email passwords to end-users or when they give out passwords to end-users over the phone. Challenge questions are customizable.

WSP also allows end-users to create their own user accounts without administrator involvement. If more complex workflow around account verification is necessary, self-registrations can be set to require either end-user confirmation (to prevent automated account creation bots) or approval by an internal user.

System Requirements

PistolStar's Password Power 8 plug-ins have the following system requirements:

Web Set Password Plug-In

- Lotus Domino 5/6/7
- Microsoft Windows NT, 2000, 2003
- IBM AIX 5.1 and higher
- IBM System i-V5R3 and higher
- All x86 Linux distributions
- Sun Solaris SPARC 8 and higher
- Lotus Sametime 3.1, 6.5.1, 7 (optional)
- Lotus QuickPlace 3.1, 6.5.1, 7 (optional)
- Domino.doc 6.5.1, 7 (optional)

Domino SSO and Authentication Redirection Plug-In

- Lotus Domino 5/6/7
- Microsoft Windows NT, 2000, 2003
- IBM AIX 5.1 and higher
- IBM System i-V5R3 and higher
- All x86 Linux distributions
- Sun Solaris SPARC 9 and higher
- LDAP Server : Microsoft Active Directory, Novell eDirectory, SunONE/ iPlanet, Domino
- SAP NetWeaver 2004 (optional)
- WebSphere 5.1+ (optional)
- WebSphere Portal 5.1+ (optional)

Single Sign-On Cookies

- Windows 2000 Professional or XP Professional
- Microsoft GINA or Novell Netware client
- Lotus Notes client 5/6/7 for Windows (optional)

For more information about PistolStar and Password Power 8 plug-ins, visit www.pistolstar.com.

CMT Inspector

Common Migration Tool (CMT) Inspector from Binary Tree gives Domino customers the real information they need about the importance/interconnectness of their Domino investment, which is critical in planning and executing changes/ additions to their infrastructure.

Before even thinking about making upgrades/additions/wholesale changes to their Domino environment, customers must have a handle on what is in place today, who's using what and how often, and so on, to justify the legacy environment (let alone future investment options).

Customers gain explicit knowledge of the complexity, depth, and inherent importance of their Domino investment today, seeing usage levels, access levels, storage levels, all amalgamated into customized reports and/or a relational database. From this information, an investment justification can be built for future Lotus leverage, including the addition of new technologies and/or potential application migrations, and so on, taking the customer to their planned application level faster with financial conviction, and a true representation of their investment's inherent value for the organization.

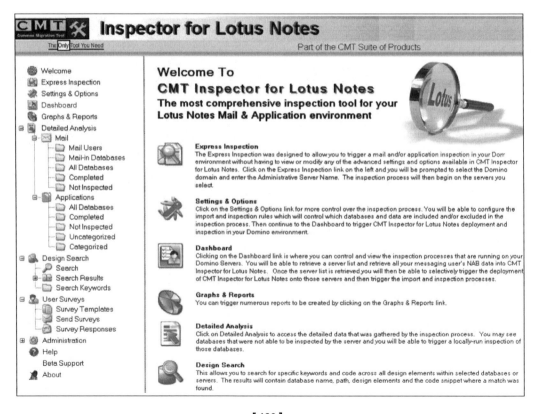

Architecture and Deployment Options

CMT Inspector can be deployed as a single database that will run interactively from the Lotus Notes client and access every specified Domino server. Alternatively, CMT Inspector can be configured to deploy a copy of itself onto specified Domino servers and to gather information via scheduled agents, resulting in significantly reduced data gathering times. Once this is complete, the data is then collected by the master database for reporting and the deployed copies are deleted.

CMT Inspector is a crawler. This allows it to gather information locally, significantly reducing analysis time. Most products are client/server based, meaning that they access all applications from one client. Imagine how long it would take to analyze a slow server in Paris from New York?

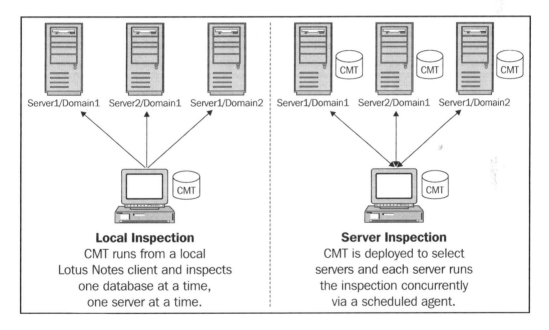

Local Inspection
CMT runs from a local
Lotus Notes client and inspects
one database at a time,
one server at a time.

Server Inspection
CMT is deployed to select
servers and each server runs
the inspection concurrently
via a scheduled agent.

CMT Inspector allows you to search for specific keywords across all design elements in your Lotus Notes applications, so you can identify specific functionality that you may want to uncover.

User surveys can be configured, distributed, and reported to gather useful information from the application's users. Surveys can be delivered to document authors/editors or based on who is in the ACL.

CMT Inspector can analyze the users' desktops to fully understand exactly which applications are being accessed via the Notes client.

Desktop Data that is Gathered:

- **Location Documents**
- **Connection Documents**
- **Replication Settings**
- **Database Icons Used**
- **Bookmarks Used**
- **Icon Location on Workspace**

CMT Inspector comes with an extensive collection of reports that are automatically generated in Excel. Furthermore, all data can be exported to Microsoft Access for further reporting and querying. This means that almost any report can be generated on the fly.

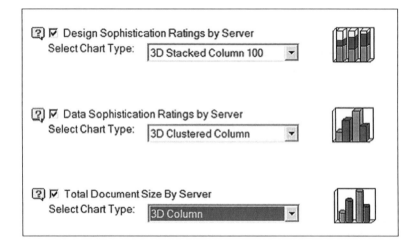

CMT for Public Folders

The Binary Tree Common Migration Tool (CMT) migrates data from one email system to another. The tool can be used to migrate from numerous email systems to Lotus Notes, and like the DUS tool CMT, has the ability to migrate both server-based data and end-user-based data.

Suppose you have business-critical information stored in Exchange Public folders and you have to migrate to Lotus Notes. How do you migrate the data in the public folders?

Binary Tree's CMT for public folder tool provides a simple and user-friendly means of migrating a public folder hierarchy to a single database, making your mail migrations from Microsoft Exchange to Lotus Domino easier.

The data in a Microsoft Exchange Public Folder often has a significant value that has been protected with permissions, based on the identities stored in the Exchange's Directory. To help companies recover the intellectual capital often found in these public folders, Binary Tree has created CMT for Exchange Public Folders. CMT not only takes data from the public folders, but can also mimic the permissions that existed on the Exchange servers in brand new Domino databases. CMT migrates the standard Exchange document types, including mail messages, calendar events, journal items, tasks, and notes. If your public folders contain forms that have been modified to include additional fields and data types, the CMT tool can be customized to migrate this data as well.

CMT for Notes

Binary Tree's Common Migration Tool for Notes builds on 13 years of outstanding email and calendar/schedule migration solutions from Binary Tree. To date, millions of users worldwide have been migrated to Lotus Notes with Binary Tree's CMT for Notes tool.

CMT for Notes offers several business benefits:

- CMT is an enterprise migration solution and can manage large migrations (up to 50,000 users have been migrated at one time). There is no limit to the number of users that can be imported from a source directory.

- Wizards set up specific functions such as importing users, registration to the Domino directory, end-user migration, and server-to-server migration.

- Mail files can be created during the registration process.

- There is date filtering for migrating mail, calendar, and tasks during an Exchange server-to-server migration.

- Processes can be rolled out into two steps: registering users and migrating them.

- Which data types are migrated – mail, calendar, notes, journal, tasks, and contacts, depending on individual needs, space, and time – can be customized.

- Schedule users and/or groups migrate at specific times, thereby limiting network load and support calls.

- Migrations do not require end-users. The administrator can perform the migration cutting down on your IT department's time and expense.

- Detailed logs with extensive error reporting help administrators to identify, interpret, and resolve issues.

CMT for Coexistence

Offloading most of the traffic from the Microsoft Exchange Notes Connector, yields more stable and reliable connectivity between Lotus Notes and Microsoft Exchange.

The most popular and highly functional connectivity solution between Microsoft Exchange and Lotus Notes environments is the Notes Connector for Microsoft Exchange. This solution addresses email, calendar and scheduling and task data exchange, automated directory synchronization, and free/busy lookup between Microsoft Exchange and Lotus Notes environments.

To overcome issues reported by many customers using the Microsoft Notes Connector, Binary Tree's solution greatly enhances fidelity of mail exchange and improves connectivity reliability. This is accomplished by the introduction of a series of configuration and programmatic changes into the environment.

Starting with Exchange 2000 and Notes 6, both products support iCal. iCal is the standard for encoding calendar messages in SMTP format. This allows email and calendaring to be sent via SMTP, which greatly offloads the stress on the Microsoft Connector and greatly improves fidelity.

What does CMT for Lotus/Exchange Coexistence Do?

Offload all mail traffic from the Microsoft Notes Connector using SMTP and MIME encoding effectively bypassing the inefficient RichText conversion used by the MS Notes Connector. MIME encoding is much more efficient preserving 100% fidelity.

Offload all calendar traffic by encoding the message in iCal format and passing it via SMTP instead of through the MS Notes Connector.

MS Notes Connector and CMT for Lotus/Exchange Coexistence

The Notes Connector on being integrated with CMT for Lotus/Exchange Coexistence provides the following:

- Directory synchronization
- Free/Busy lookups
- Never crashes and have the ability to scale to an unlimited amount of users

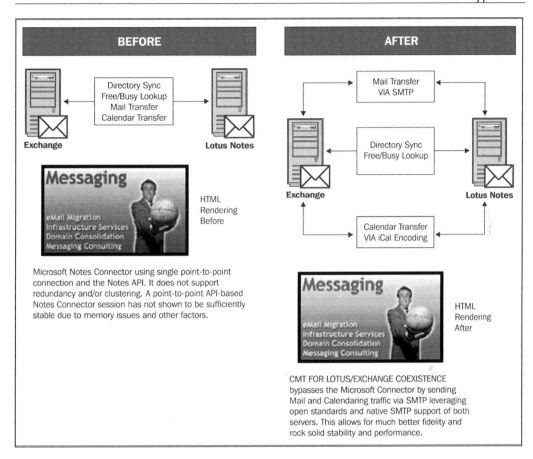

CMT for Domains

Your Domain infrastructure is a vital asset and should be protected. Your IT environment is unique, and you need something designed with adaptability in mind.

CMT for Domains, Users, Servers, and Desktops is a solution that expedites the conversion between platforms while diminishing the bearing on your IT resources. A user-friendly administrator tool requiring virtually no end-user interaction, CMT for Domains, Servers, Users, and Desktops, will enable you to automate the entire migration life cycle in minutes.

Utilizing CMT for Domains, Servers, Users, and Desktops, the following processes can be accomplished with the click of a button:

- *Entire Environment and User Audit*: Wholly automates the replacement of users' present naming structure with the new one.

- *All-encompassing Jurisdiction of the Migration Process*: This provides the administrator a complete overview of the migration life-cycle, providing meticulous data with process information (based on migration phases of users).

- *Instigates the renaming of multiple users to the new hierarchical name/upgrade*: The practice of migrating and/or consolidating Lotus Notes Domains is habitually escorted by altering end-users' hierarchical naming structures. Commonly, a Lotus Notes Administrator performs the process of Lotus Notes Domain migration by using a multifaceted, lingering process provided by Lotus. CMT for Domains, Users, Servers, and Desktops condenses this process and accomplishes the task quickly and efficiently with the minimal amount of effort.

Notes Desktop Update

The Notes Desktop Update is programmed as an email message containing a button for each user to click. Users' desktop information (server names for databases, user accesses, mail file and personal address book, location documents, connection documents, and so on) are automatically updated with the new infrastructure information with one click.

Notes Port

The Notes Port runs on the Domino server and, by design, replaces all reference to each migrated user's old infrastructure information with the new one in the users mail database. (This includes fields in mail messages, calendar, meetings, and to-dos.)

Other Features

In addition, CMT Inspector offers the following features:

- Moving users/applications to a different Notes Domain/Domino Server and amending the Domino Directory to reflect the move.
- Monitoring the rename process.
- Monitoring the move progress.
- No more digging through help files looking for answers.

Never before has a consolidation of multiple Lotus Notes Domains been more straight-forward. CMT consists of everything a Lotus Notes Administrator needs to move users from an existing domain to a new one. Furthermore, as a result of the migration using CMT, users will appear to have always lived on the new domain.

FT Search Manager

IONET FT Search Manager is a Lotus Notes based search tool for Lotus Notes and Domino environments. The product uses standard Lotus Notes technologies, but in an innovative way. The FT Search Manager supersedes the native Lotus Search Site and Domain Search functions by providing user-targeted searching of any database, in any location without building central search indexes. This gives maximum effectiveness, speed, flexibility, and security to the user. As an example, the user can securely search for the content of a specific field across six encrypted local mail archives, their server-based mail file, and 12 other databases on different servers worldwide. The user selects only databases that have content relevant to them, and they can customize the results individually (or the administrator can do it for them). In addition, they can perform common search functions, such as Google-style searching, and searching within results. For the full product description, features, and downloads, visit `http://www.ionetsoftware.com/ftsearch`.

In any Lotus Notes/Domino environment of R6 and greater, the capabilities described below are available. They are summarized as:

- *Multi-threading in the Notes client* utilizes the full potential of the Notes client by working in parallel and not sequentially.

- *Emulating browser behavior* allows your users to just hit *Enter* to start searching (you don't need to go get your mouse and click a button). Also no more "Lotus AND Notes AND NOT Microsoft" type queries. Use "Lotus +Notes -Microsoft" instead, as you do in your favorite web search engine.

Let's look at these in more detail.

Multi-Threading in the Notes Client

The FT Search Manager starts ten multi-threaded agents in parallel. All agents start at the same time and run simultaneously. For example, if five databases are being searched, Agents 1-5 search one database each, and Agents 6-10 do nothing. If 12 databases are searched, Agent 1 searches databases 1 and 11, Agent 2 searches databases 2 and 12, Agent 3 searches Database 3, Agent 4 searches Database 4, and so on. There is nothing particularly clever about these agents, they are all normal LotusScript agents with the "Run in Background Client Thread" setting selected, and they are all started at the same time.

The benefits of multi-threading agents are described in the following sections.

Speed

The following tests are a comparison of running the agents in parallel vs. running them sequentially. The only difference between the tests is that in the sequential test, the "Run in Background Client Thread" setting is deselected, forcing sequential operation.

The tests were run on the R7.01 server and client version, with the client searching 20 databases, totaling approximately 60 MB. Each agent searched two databases, finding and processing 100 document results per database, and formatting these in HTML for display to the user. This is a total of 2000 results per search.

Parallel agent results:

Agent1 Start: 14:31:05:36

Agent1 End: 14:31:11:14

Agent2 Start: 14:31:05:36

Agent2 End: 14:31:10:94

Agent3 Start: 14:31:05:32

Agent3 End: 14:31:09:86

Agent4 Start: 14:31:05:37

Agent4 End: 14:31:10:16

Agent5 Start: 14:31:05:37

Agent5 End: 14:31:11:14

Agent6 Start: 14:31:05:38

Agent6 End: 14:31:10:79

Agent7 Start: 14:31:05:33

Agent7 End: 14:31:11:14

Agent8 Start: 14:31:05:39

Agent8 End: 14:31:10:87

Agent9 Start: 14:31:05:39

Agent9 End: 14:31:11:14

Agent10 Start: 14:31:05:40

Agent10 End: 14:31:11:14

Note that all agents started within a second of each other and completed within six seconds. Agent 3 was the first agent to finish—as there is no correlation between the agents, search results appear "as they arrive". In reality this means that smaller local databases usually display their results first, while results from larger remote databases are the last to arrive. As the client is searching in the background, the user can read the initial results, or even other information like mail, while all the results arrive.

The same ten agents were then rerun, with the only change being that it was not multi-threaded (deselect "Run in Client Background Thread"):

Sequential agent results:

Agent1 Start: 15:35:33:32

Agent1 End: 15:35:34:28

Agent2 Start: 15:35:34.47

Agent2 End: 15:35:35.52

Agent3 Start: 15:35:35.75

Agent3 End: 15:35:36.59

Agent4 Start: 15:35:36.80

Agent4 End: 15:35:37.66

Agent5 Start: 15:35:37.86

Agent5 End: 15:35:38.70

Agent6 Start: 15:35:38.90

Agent6 End: 15:35:39.58

Agent7 Start: 15:35:39.88

Agent7 End: 15:35:40.79

Agent8 Start: 15:35:40.98

Agent8 End: 15:35:41.85

Agent9 Start: 15:35:42.05

Agent9 End: 15:35:42.88

Agent10 Start: 15:35:43.07

Agent10 End: 15:35:43.73

Note how the agents run sequentially, starting one after the other, and completing within 10 seconds. This can be seen in the following chart:

CMT Inspector for Lotus offers you the capability to search for specific keywords across all design elements in your Lotus Notes Applications in order to identify specific functionality that you may want to uncover.

User surveys can be configured, distributed, and reported on to gather useful information from the application's users. Surveys can be delivered to document authors/edits or based on who is in the ACL.

The following results were obtained over ten consecutive searches (showing elapsed time for all agents to complete, in seconds):

Run #	1	2	3	4	5	6	7	8	9	10	Av.
Parallel	5.37	5.66	5.34	6.11	5.81	5.73	5.93	5.70	5.82	5.54	5.70
Serial	9.69	9.41	9.27	9.44	9.52	9.22	9.53	9.38	9.38	9.77	9.46

This shows that over ten runs, the parallel agents were 66% faster than the sequential agents. This can be seen in the following chart:

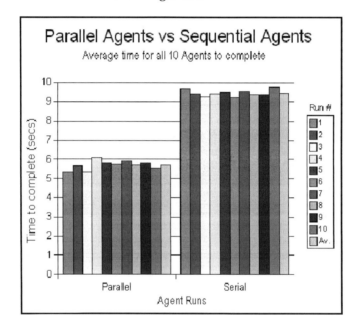

Concurrent Client Operation

As concurrent agents are run in the background, you can use your client for other functions. For instance you can read the results from the first two databases, while the remaining 18 populate in the background. You can even do something completely different, such as read mail. The screen shot below shows a client searching at the same time as the user is reading his or her mail.

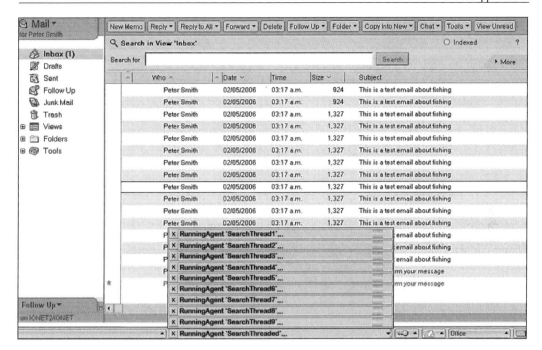

Code Locking

Code locking (CodeLock/CodeUnLock) statements are generally only used in the Lotus world when running concurrent web agents on a Domino server to perform some function where unique access is required to an object (for instance, incrementing a hit counter in a specific document). Code locking is not used in the standard Agent Manager Run agents, as it is only effective within the same process—the Agent Manager often starts more than one executive (process), so code locking is redundant. Server-run agents initiated from the web run via an Agent Manager add-in, not the Agent Manager, so they run within a single process. In the same way, when a Notes client starts multiple concurrent agents using the "Run in Background Client Thread" setting, all agents run in the same process, so code locking can be successfully used.

If you want to access common objects when using multiple agents (for example to increment counters in a document), you should use the CodeLock LotusScript statements to lock access to the object while using it. This is mandatory to provide a consistent result (for example, setting a counter), and it's also very useful in avoiding client crashes. As long as the scripts are coded to minimize time spent on using the common objects (freeing the locks as soon as possible), this doesn't have a detrimental affect on performance. The take-home message is that if you think there might be contentious use of an object (database, view, document and so on), then lock it.

The following is an example of code locking:

```
Dim s as new NotesSession
Dim db as NotesDatabase
Dim doc as NotesDocument
Dim lockID as Integer
Dim lockStatus as Integer

'***GET LOCK
lockID = Createlock("SearchLock")
Do While True
    If Codelock(lockID) Then
        Exit Do            '  Got the lock, exit Loop
    End If
Loop

Set db = s.CurrentDatabase
docID$ = xxxx            'set Document Unique ID
Set doc = db.GetDocumentByUNID(docID$)
If doc.HasItem("Counter") Then
    docNo% = resultHeader.Counter(0)
    docNo% = docNo% + 1
    doc.Counter = docNo%
Else
    doc.Counter = 1
End If
Call doc.Save(True, True, True)

'***END LOCK
lockStatus = Codeunlock(lockID) ' Let other agents get the lock
lockStatus = Destroylock(lockID) ' Destroy the lock of there
                                 are no more agents waiting
```

More information and examples about locking code can be found in the Domino Designer online Help.

Emulating Browser Behavior

Two common complaints about Notes-based searching is users having to start searching by clicking a button (not just pressing *Enter*), and having to remember a Notes-based query syntax. These are covered below.

A Workaround to the Notes "Enter" Problem

In Notes search applications (in fact, this commonly applies to any application), the user has to type in their search query, then find the mouse and click a **Search** button. Alternatively, they can tab to the button and press *Space*. This is different from browser-based searching where the user types in their query and then just presses *Enter* to begin the search. This workaround uses a JavaScript timer to locate a Carriage Return in a field, perform an action based on its existence, and then removes it.

The timing in milliseconds can be decreased (shown here as 100 ms, or 1/10 of a second), but at a cost to the processing percentage used by the client (as the client is continually checking the required field).

All events are Client Javascript. "*YourSearchField*" means the field the cursor is in when the user can just press *Enter* to click a button (begin a search). For example this might be called "Query". "*YourButton*" means the button whose code will be executed when the user presses *Enter*.

YourSearchField onFocus event:

```
// Check every 1/10 of a second
useClick = window.setInterval("runSearch()",100);
```

YourSearchField onBlur event:

```
window.clearInterval(useClick);
```

YourButton: The button (in this example) requires an HTML Name of "*Button*". This is set on the HTML tab of the button properties dialog.

Form JS Header:

```
var newline = String.fromCharCode(10);
var useClick;
var sString;
var t_sString;

function runSearch() {
sString = document.forms[0].YourSearchField.value;
if (sString.indexOf(newline)>=0) {
t_sString = replace(sString, '\n', '');
document.forms[0].YourSearchField.value = t_sString;
document.forms[0].elements['Button'].click();
}
}

function replace(str, from, to) {
var i = str.indexOf(from);
```

```
if (!from || !str || i == -1) return str;
var newstr = str.substring(0, i) + to;
if ·(i+from.length < str.length)
newstr += replace(str.substring(i+from.length,str.length),from,to);
return newstr;
}
```

You may see the client add a line to your Query and then remove it, but remember that this is just a workaround until something better comes along.

Allowing Web-Style Query Syntax

It is confusing for users to use different search query syntax when using Notes instead of the same syntax they use when Web searching. For instance, see the following Google search:

```
"no-code" -Javascript java "trackback client" OR
re-entered+array+string+it
```

This would be represented in Notes as:

```
NOT "no-code" AND NOT "Javascript" AND java AND "trackback client"
OR re-entered AND array AND string AND "it"
```

The FT Search Manager uses text parsing to translate web-style queries into Notes syntax, displaying the web-style query to the user while internally using the Notes-style query. This ensures that your users don't need to remember two different search syntaxes.

This procedure is too complicated to show here, but it can be roughly summarized as:

1. Create an array of all of the search words by splitting the query using " ".
2. For each element in the array, replace web search operators (+, -, and so on) with the relevant Notes operator (AND, AND NOT), taking care to recognize quoted strings and strings containing operators, for example "re-entered".
3. Reassemble the query in the Notes syntax making liberal use of parentheses.

For a working example of this LotusScript function, please contact IONET.

About IONET

IONET are a Wellington, New Zealand based company that have specialized in Lotus Notes and Domino solutions since V3.0 (circa 1993). They concentrate on innovative, low-cost products to enhance the usability of any Lotus Notes/Domino environment.

For more information on IONET or its products, visit:

http://www.ionetsoftware.com.

Index

code, reviewing 77
final note 79
new templates, customizing 77
script libraries, recompiling 77, 78
Tivoli Autonomic Monitoring Engine.
    See **TAME**

U

UDDI
about 101
registry 133
Universal Description Discovery and
    Integration. *See* **UDDI**

V

vendor tools
Angkor 175-179
CMT Inspector 186
FT Search Manager 193
PistolStar Password Power 8 179
views
about 136, 137
categorized columns 138
Reader Names 139, 140
storing in variable, advantages 142
time/date 138, 139
view size, reducing 137

W

web services
about 101
CompanyInfo implementing, Java used
    122-129

complex return types 118-122
creating, Domino designer 7 used 103-105
exception handling, adding 112, 113
expanding to include complex data types
    114-118
exploring, browser used 107-112
implementing 105
need for Domino 102
Rational Application Developer's Web
    Services Explorer 108
SOAP, technologies used 101
technologies used 101
UDDI, technologies used 101
UDDI registry 133
WSDL, technologies used 101
WSDL actions, Domino Designer 7 130
XML, technologies used 101
WSDL
about 101
actions 130-132
export 130
import 131, 132
show 132

X

XML 101

Thank you for buying
Domino 7 Application Development

About Packt Publishing

Packt, pronounced 'packed', published its first book "*Mastering phpMyAdmin for Effective MySQL Management*" in April 2004 and subsequently continued to specialize in publishing highly focused books on specific technologies and solutions.

Our books and publications share the experiences of your fellow IT professionals in adapting and customizing today's systems, applications, and frameworks. Our solution based books give you the knowledge and power to customize the software and technologies you're using to get the job done. Packt books are more specific and less general than the IT books you have seen in the past. Our unique business model allows us to bring you more focused information, giving you more of what you need to know, and less of what you don't.

Packt is a modern, yet unique publishing company, which focuses on producing quality, cutting-edge books for communities of developers, administrators, and newbies alike. For more information, please visit our website: www.packtpub.com.

Writing for Packt

We welcome all inquiries from people who are interested in authoring. Book proposals should be sent to authors@packtpub.com. If your book idea is still at an early stage and you would like to discuss it first before writing a formal book proposal, contact us; one of our commissioning editors will get in touch with you.

We're not just looking for published authors; if you have strong technical skills but no writing experience, our experienced editors can help you develop a writing career, or simply get some additional reward for your expertise.

Upgrading to Lotus Notes and Domino 7

ISBN: 1-904811-63-9   Paperback: 320 pages

Upgrade your company to the latest version of Lotus Notes and Domino.

1. Understand the new features and put them to work in your business

2. Appreciate the implications of changes and new features

3. Learn how to integrate Lotus Notes/Domino 7 with WebSphere and Microsoft Outlook

4. A real-life case study of how Lotus upgraded its own developerWorks site to Lotus Notes/Domino 7

Business Process Execution Language for Web Services 2nd Edition

ISBN: 1-904811-81-7   Paperback: 350 pages

An Architects and Developers Guide to BPEL and BPEL4WS.

1. Architecture, syntax, development and composition of Business Processes and Services using BPEL

2. Advanced BPEL features such as compensation, concurrency, links, scopes, events, dynamic partner links, and correlations

3. Oracle BPEL Process Manager and BPEL Designer Microsoft BizTalk Server as a BPEL server

Please check **www.PacktPub.com** for information on our titles

Alfresco Enterprise Content Management Implementation

ISBN: 1-904811-11-6   Paperback: 240 pages

How to Install, use, and customize this powerful, free, Open Source Java-based Enterprise CMS.

1. **Manage your business documents**: version control, library services, content organization, and search

2. **Workflows and business rules**: move and manipulate content automatically when events occur

3. **Maintain, extend, and customize Alfresco**: backups and other admin tasks, customizing and extending the content model, creating your own look and feel

Programming Windows Workflow Foundation: Practical WF Techniques and Examples using XAML and C#

ISBN: 1-904811-21-3   Paperback: 300 pages

A C# developer's guide to the features and programming interfaces of Windows Workflow Foundation.

1. Add event-driven workflow capabilities to your .NET applications

2. Highlights the libraries, services and internals programmers need to know

3. Builds a practical "bug reporting" workflow solution example app

Please check **www.PacktPub.com** for information on our titles